D0375953

PEOPLE

The "Our Alberta Heritage" Series

By Jacques Hamilton

Illustrated by Tom Nelson

COMMISSIONED BY CALGARY POWER LTD.
CALGARY, ALBERTA, CANADA

Copyright © Calgary Power Ltd.
FIRST PRINTING, MAY, 1971
SECOND PRINTING, JULY, 1971

Printed in Canada

INTRODUCTION

The history of Alberta has always fascinated me.

It is in this province that I have spent my business life; it is here that I raised a family and it is here that I have witnessed the events of history grow into a proud heritage for the one and one-half million people who call Alberta home.

It was just over 60 years ago when a small power generating plant, 50 miles west of Calgary, began delivering electricity to a handful of customers. That plant, Horseshoe Falls, was owned and operated by the Calgary Power Company Limited, the forerunner of what is now Calgary Power Ltd. Since that time Calgary Power has been intimately connected with Alberta and its heritage.

And so it is not unusual that we should have a deep interest in history. To commemorate our 60th anniversary, May 21, 1971, we commissioned the research and writing of this book series, based on the history of Alberta. We realized that a detailed chronology of Alberta was not what we wanted. We felt it important to capture the spirit of Alberta's early life, rather than a year-by-year account of events. And so as you read the following pages you will see that our author, Jacques Hamilton, has considered the history of the province as a series of anecdotes and stories drawn from the lives of those who contributed to Alberta's past.

In this volume Mr. Hamilton takes a look at the PEOPLE who made Alberta. While history is really nothing more than people, we place special emphasis on the character and fortitude of those pioneers who engraved their names into our heritage.

The stories between the covers of this volume are filled with happiness and sadness, hardship and reward, triumph and failure. At the same time they are all laced with the determination and ambition that gave Alberta pioneers a special place in Canadian history.

But, as we discovered in our research, this determination to improve and develop did not end at some point in the past. Today's Albertans have the same dedication to building and growing . . . indeed leaders today in most walks of life will find a legitimate place in Alberta's future chronicles of pioneers.

We at Calgary Power trust that you will find the same enjoyment in reading these stories as we have experienced in finding and recording them.

— G. H. Thompson
Chairman of the Board
Calgary Power Ltd.

It is impossible to name them all here, but we would like to express our gratitude to the hundreds of Albertans who so graciously gave their time, their help and their rare records to make this project possible. There are two other people we would like to thank particularly: Mrs. Edith Smith of Calgary and Mrs. Naomi Radford of Edmonton. Without their efforts, these books could never have been completed.

— J. H.

CONTENTS

CHURCHMEN

BEENY, DISCIPLE OF ZAZEEKRY . . .

The first black-robed missionaries struggled westward to what is now Alberta in search of heathens to convert.

They found heathens, all right, but they also found a surprise waiting for them. Sheltered in the foothills of the Rockies, completely isolated from white men, they found a tribe of Indians practising a distorted but recognizable form of Christianity.

The missionaries heard of the Indians' god and Zazeekry — a figure astonishingly close to the Christian Christ. They heard of angels, of baptism, and they saw with their own eyes the cross that was the symbol of the tribe's religion.

And soon they heard the name of Beeny, the Indian seer who had brought his people this new religion and who was probably the west's first "missionary" — though hardly in the Christian sense of the word.

Stunned, the missionaries dismissed Beeny and his religion as tools of the "Dark Spirit". But, at the same time, goaded by curiosity, they investigated what they had found, and uncovered a story as strange as any to come out of the west.

The story they uncovered had begun some years earlier, during a snow-bound February.

Since fall, Beeny had hidden himself in his hunting lodge. He was said to be sick, but there were many of his tribe who suggested he was only sick with mortification at being put to shame by an arch-rival in the yearly witchcraft contest.

The rival, a sorcerer named Gustlee, had dumbfounded the gathered tribes by emerging from the earth as a ghost, accompanied by a dreaded monster, the Double-Headed-Snake. At his sudden appearance, a number of his followers had "fallen dead" with fear, and Gustlee had used his magic to bring them back to life.

The trick of "resurrection" was one Beeny had heard of, but had never been able to master, and he could not bear the thought that his hated rival had managed to conquer its secrets.

Beeny's defeat at the hands of Gustlee had been a disgrace. It had shamed him before the assembled tribes, and Beeny had taken to the cedar mat inside his lodge rather than show his face in daylight.

Long before spring, however, those who had questioned Beeny's illness had cause to reconsider. Word had come from the seer's lodge that he was on the point of death.

"He has not long to live now," the messengers claimed; "a green fluid is streaming out of his mouth and he is unable to speak."

As the Indians told the missionaries years later, the ailment was strange indeed. Beeny had continued to waste away. After the green fluid had flowed from his mouth, he would be lifted into mid-air as if his body had become as light as a leaf. It was difficult at times to hold him down to his couch.

At nights, they claimed, Beeny would rise from the ground and walk along the walls like a beetle or under the roof like a fly.

In desperation, Beeny's tribe even summoned his hated enemy Gustlee to try to save him. Gustlee, however, was not even granted entry to the lodge.

Enraged, Gustlee warned the frightened gathering that "Beeny is too ill to recover. Shame and jealousy have gnawed at his heart. He shall die! That is what I have to say."

Gustlee's prediction soon came true. Or at least it seemed to come true.

One morning, the tribesmen discovered that Beeny had simply disappeared from his mat in the lodge.

Outside, there were tracks in the snow, leading off to the woods. The Indians followed the trail, but it gradually faded, disappearing entirely at a spot where dozens of trees had been violently uprooted, plucked from the earth and scattered as though by some giant hand in the sky.

In the remains of one pine tree, the followers found Beeny's clothes. "Strange," they muttered as they looked around fearfully, "he has died and gone up into the sky against his will."

There, but for Beeny's relatives, it might have ended. They, instead of accepting the seer's death, stubbornly insisted that "He is not dead, he has only gone up."

Refusing to go into the required deep mourning, they pressed on in the search for the missing Beeny.

Summer passed, then another winter, and a new spring, but still the relatives refused to hold the funeral rites.

Suddenly, in May, Beeny was found; apparently dead.

The women of the tribe had been out gathering pine sap, and had come to the edge of a clearing where it looked as though monsters had held a war. Holes had been torn in the ground and the forest was a jumble. Trees had been thrust, upside down, into the ground.

Horrified, the women fled back to the village and roused the men who snatched up weapons and raced to the spot.

Like the women, they hung back, terrified, on the edge of the clearing. Then, one of the men, squinting upward suddenly yelled: "Look! There is a body."

The rest of the men focussed on the tree. There was, indeed, something wedged in the fork high off the ground, but none could tell if it was human or animal.

Reluctantly, the men decided to chop down the tree.

As they began battering the base of the trunk with their stone axes, a board came clattering down; a piece of cedar covered with signs and scrolls in black and red.

Although uneasy, they chopped on and minutes later a white cloth decorated with shiny discs fluttered to their feet. None of the men had ever seen anything like it before.

The tree was on the point of falling when a ghostly, whistling voice was heard from overhead and the men dropped their axes and fled.

Some time later, when a trace of courage had returned, the men came back to the clearing. A body had fallen from the tree and was buried to its waist in the ground. Face and hands painted white, skin as dry as buckskin, it was the corpse of Beeny.

As soon as the body was laid within Beeny's lodge, mourning began. For three days, as the number of criers, singers and dancers grew, the camp was filled with the moaning funeral dirge:

"We are near the cave of the dead, the cave of the dead

. . . The trail is bad, we fear we are lost . . . Here we have come to the dark river . . ."

Then, on the third day, something strange happened inside the funeral lodge and the camp fell silent. Those beside the body had heard the scroll-covered board creak and sizzle, and had heard four distinct rapping sounds.

Just before sunset, a youth whose skin and hair had been white from birth crept into the lodge and sat beside the body. He stared at Beeny for a long time, listening closely.

"I hear something," he whispered. "I hear him singing, inside his body."

No one else could hear anything. But the youth was insistent. "So it is, I hear his voice, I hear his song, Hahaee-he neebahu-dju tisnahay . . ."

Gradually, as time went by, others in the lodge began to hear the song coming from inside Beeny's lifeless body. The song grew steadily louder and more distinct.

The youth began to hum the song vibrating in the corpse, and soon others were humming as well. Then the youth began to sing Beeny's song and, in minutes, the whole camp was singing in unison. "Hahaee-he neebahu-dju . . ."

In the hours that followed, the amazed watchers saw faint stirrings in Beeny's body, saw him begin to breathe. Slowly, as the spectators gasped, Beeny sat up. Then he stood.

Beeny had come back to life; he had resurrected himself.

Up to this point, the story of Beeny did not alarm the skeptical missionaries particularly. It was clearly just a case of a skilled sorcerer taking much time, and going to great lengths of trickery, to outdo a hated rival.

But as the story continued, the missionaries found much to disturb them:

Beeny, when he opened his mouth to speak, dumbfounded his listeners. His words were like nothing they had ever heard before. They could not understand him at all.

But the sorcerer had anticipated the problem. Beeny drew the white-haired youth to him, pressed a bone in each ear and rubbed saliva on the boy's brow.

Beeny had given the youth the power to understand him, and from that point until Beeny "relearned" his own language, the boy would be his disciple and interpreter.

Beeny and his disciple went outside the next morning to face the hundreds of Indians who had gathered from near and far to see him. As the youth interpreted, the seer told his story:

"My body was sore to the point of crumbling away many moons ago. Then I saw a ladder alongside my body, a ladder reaching up from my cedar mat into the sky. A voice at the top called me up; that is why I started to climb.

"When I looked down I stood at the tree tops. I tried to touch them with my right hand; that is how the trees were pulled out of the ground. Brothers and friends, have you seen the trees uprooted?"

There was a murmur of acknowledgment from the people before him. Beeny continued.

"I dropped my raiment, I dropped it and it fell upon the limbs of a tree. Was it lost or was it found?"

"We found it on the limbs of a tree," one of the crowd replied.

Beeny nodded. "I climbed the ladder for a night and a day. It was only my shade that was climbing, for my body was left behind. It fell between the forks of a tree. It was dead.

"I could not get into the sky all at once, only little by little. My shade pierced the sky vault slowly, slowly, even as a new-born child comes slowly into this world. When I was half-way above, I beheld the four corners of Heaven.

"At the point where the sun sets was a very old man, as tall as a tree, as white as snow. Many, oh so many people, all pale-faced, sat everywhere, but they were all like wood carvings, mute and motionless. No one took any notice of me.

"Then I turned to the east and beheld the spirits with white garments who stood near the opening where the sun rises every morning. They alone in sky-land moved their hands, their feet, their faces and their bodies as we do. In their hands they were beating skin drums while they danced in circles and sang, 'Sun, good Sun, when is it that you began to rise and set in the sky?' "

Beeny paused to rest, and, when the sun rose, continued his story.

"This is the second day of the shortest span of time (the week)," Beeny said. "I shall tell you of the two head-chiefs of the Sky, the Father and the Son.

"The name of the Father is Old Man. He has always been, he is as ancient as the world. Yet he cannot die, for he is a manitou, the oldest sky manitou.

"Listen to his song, brothers and friends. It is a wonderful song, the song of the Old Man: 'Since the world first grew I have lived until now. Old as I am, I remain strong. The manitous of the mountain peaks, the manitous of the canyons, the manitou of the wind, the manitou of the trees and the waters are all in me. From them, from all nature, I am strong, I am everlasting. I can give life again. Those who sing my song shall stand up from amongst the dead, . . ."

The crowd, excited by the words of the song, began to hum, then to sing.

As they sang, Beeny retired to his lodge and resumed his trance.

The next morning, however, he appeared again. On his left arm he carried the white cloth with the shining discs. At his feet lay a horn bowl filled with clear water.

"This is the third day of the short span," he said, then touched his forehead with his right hand, then touched each shoulder and his breast. Everyone in the crowd imitated him in making the Sign of the Cross.

"Listen," Beeny continued, "my dream now was of the Son, Zazeekry, who stands next to Old Man among the Sky manitous, and holds a tree (the cross) and a bowl of water in his hands. This is what the manitou Zazeekry told me, 'Very soon a great plague shall visit your people. The earth shall crumble to pieces and fire shall leap out of the ground, and the big sky monster shall swallow the sun and the moon. Darkness and smoke shall prevail everywhere.

" 'Go and tell your people! They are all sinners. They are not baptized, they know nothing of my Cross, they do not marry in the proper way, and when they die, their bodies are hung in the trees, then burned to charcoal on the pyre.

" 'Your people are bad, they are heathens. That is why the earth shall break up and burn to cinders.'

"Then Zazeekry poured the water of baptism from his bowl on to my head, and he said, 'Beeny — Mind-all-over-the-world — this shall be your name, for you are the first to discover who I am.

" 'You must go down the sky-ladder and return to earth, to save your tribe, your tribe and all the tribes that welcome the Truth. Baptize the people, give them new names, tell them to repent and show them the right way.'

"Then I travelled all around the sky. I stood at the four corners of the world and learned the new ways of life. The time came for me to return to you, my people. I sang the song of Old Man, the song of life, Hahaee-he neebahu-dju . . ."

All through the following days of the "short span" (the Christian week), the people of the tribe and of tribes all around rushed to Beeny to be baptized. And to listen as he continued preaching the message of Zazeekry:

"You shall not kill, you shall not lie, you shall not steal, you shall not have more than one wife, and you shall observe deemawse (dimanche, Sunday)."

Beeny also showed his followers the three "magic" gifts he said he had brought back from the sky.

The first was the white cloth he had carried on his arm while preaching. "This," he explained, "is the white cloth of Heaven. It is a blessing, for it shall cure diseases and drive away the big plague."

The second was a small board covered with peculiar colored signs. "Now behold the prayer board! Here are the seven notches, the days of the short span. You shall work six days and rest on the seventh. That is what Zazeekry does. So you must do.

"Here are the signs (the Scriptures). You shall look at them, for you must all pray and be saved from the big fire."

Then Beeny pulled out a small spruce tree carved to represent a cross. "This is the Cross of Heaven, the Cross of Penance. When you see it you must repent, you must do penance. A ten days' fast, that is what you must observe before you begin the big Indian dances."

Beeny's religion caught on quickly among the Indians of the mountain tribes. Even traditional enemies — thanks to

Beeny's ability as a magician — were converted. In one case, Beeny used a convenient eclipse of the sun to make such a tribe see the light.

But Beeny and his growing number of disciples became too lavish in their claims of the power of the new religion. As years went by, the Indians were encouraged to abandon hunting and gathering berries in favor of continuous worship.

Inevitably famine struck and, with it, disenchantment. Encouraged by Beeny's enemy Gustlee, among others, thousands turned their backs on the faith of the Sky People, and returned to their old beliefs.

Beeny himself lived long enough to hear condemnation of him by the first missionaries as "a juggler, an imposter, a servant of the Evil Spirit."

Broken-hearted, the old sorcerer died a few weeks later. This time for good.

Historians, like the early missionaries, have always been at a loss to explain the uncanny accuracy of Beeny's visions of Christianity. Perhaps the most plausible explanation is that offered by Marius Barbeau in his book, Indian Days in the Canadian Rockies:

"The wonder of it all is that this event antedated the labours of missionaries, even the appearance of the earliest white men along the perilous trails of the northern uplands.

"How could a seer like Beeny, in the vastness of his remote country, dream of heaven, baptize neophytes and establish pseudo-Christian ethics in a manner which reminds one more of a Catholic missionary than a pagan of the mountains?

"Time rubs off many connecting links, distance obscures our perception, and it is not possible yet to unravel the puzzle.

"Beeny, in his prolonged absence after his disappearance, may have travelled to some distant point, though not as far as the trade outposts. From the very impurity of his mystic notions, from his tale of marvels, it seems more likely that in the beginning at least, he laboured under the delusions of hearsay.

"Many stories from the lips of other Indians, of catholicized half-breeds from the east — Cree or Iroquois — and of French coureurs-des-bois may have reached his ears, possibly through the 'free hunters' who resorted by the score to the Rocky Mountains even before the time when Thompson, in 1807, first wintered at Lake Windermere.

"A stimulus once provided, his imagination may also have elaborated other themes about the coming of the white people — 'the sky beings' as he called them — which must have filtered through the mountain passes at a very early date."

Whatever the source of the vision, and however sad its failure, even the early Jesuits acknowledged that it eased the way for true Christian teaching among the Indians.

And so Beeny, that wily and misguided sorcerer, earned his place in history as Alberta's first missionary . . .

* * * *

THE "BIG CHIEF OF THE PRAIRIES". . .

It was 1852, and Chief Factor Rowand — volatile chief of the Hudson's Bay post at Fort Edmonton — was leading a string of loaded York boats west.

In the party, keeping well out of Rowand's way, was a young French-Canadian priest who was to become the resident churchman in the western post.

The priest, still a stranger to the west, was filled with

sympathy for the voyageurs whose unhappy task it was to haul the York boats upriver by brute strength. Strapped into harness like dray horses, they scrambled over rocks, through swamps and sometimes waded up to their armpits in the icy water.

As a French-Canadian himself, the young priest became close friends with many of the suffering boatmen.

Suddenly, one day, the young priest made an infuriating intrusion on the chief factor. One of the voyageurs, the priest informed him, was sick and barely able to stand in his harness. The man should be allowed to rest and should be given proper food.

Rowand's Irish temper boiled. How dare this callow priest

interfere with his party? And how dare one of his men complain of illness?

Those within earshot of the argument that followed were astonished to find the young priest every bit as stubborn as Rowand, and finally to hear the factor grudgingly give way.

"Give him some of your food if you must," Rowand snapped, "but he needs no rest. Any man who is not dead with three days' illness is not sick at all."

Many days later, in Fort Edmonton, Rowand had cause to recall that argument and his angry words.

Rowand had injured one of his fingers painfully and had gone to the priest — the closest figure the post had to a doctor. The priest did what he could, then sent the factor back to his own quarters with the comment: "You are not suffering, Rowand!"

Three days later, with Rowand still in agony, the priest paid him a visit. As he wrote later:

"I had to say what was in my mind, though I feared trouble might come of it. I had to touch that man of iron.

"I went to him and said — not that I was sorry, but — 'You will understand what I mean, my friend, when I tell you that you are not sick. Three days have passed now, and you are not dead. So of course you are not sick; it is all imagination.'

"His face took on an awful cloud. If I had not been his friend and a priest, I believe he would have struck me. Hah! He was like a can of powder, that little man!"

It was Rowand's first encounter with Father Albert Lacombe, that gentle but stubborn priest destined to become one of the greatest — if not the greatest — figures in Alberta history.

The little "black-robe", with the blood of an Ojibway

chief and of the voyageurs in his veins, symbolizes — more than any other man — the history that turned Alberta from a raw wilderness to a modern province.

Father Lacombe created a Cree dictionary, a Blackfoot dictionary. He built the first bridge in the west, and the first flour mill. Single-handedly he broke the transportation monopoly of the Hudson's Bay Company and introduced the Red River Cart as the main method of moving goods across the prairies.

Time and again, all alone, he stepped in to stop the carnage of the never-ending war between Cree and Blackfoot. Alone, on one occasion, he saved Fort Edmonton from an overwhelming Indian attack.

Alone, during the nightmare days of the Riel rebellion, he was able to keep the Blackfoot at peace, and thus save Alberta's white pioneers from what might have been terrible slaughter.

Without complaint, he undertook the pride-crushing task of begging through eastern Canada, the United States and Europe for the money needed to keep the vital western missions going.

The same audacity that led him to the confrontation with Rowand led him, in later years, to take on the Canadian Parliament and the Quebec press over the issue of separate schools. Once, it led him to brusquely interrupt a conversation between an archbishop and the Emperor of Austria — a diplomatic blunder that no one but Father Lacombe could have got away with.

It would be futile to attempt here the biography of this great man. That task has already been lovingly accomplished by Katherine Hughes in her book, "Father Lacombe, The Black-Robe Voyageur".

Instead, we offer a glimpse of the "Big Chief of the

Prairies" at his bravest and most-loving.

It was 1865, 13 years after Father Lacombe had first come to Alberta. All those long years he had labored among the Cree, bringing them religion and a sense of civilization.

For his efforts, he had earned the undying respect of these northern Indians. And from them he had earned an Indian name: Kamiyo-atchakwe — The Man-of-the-Beautiful Soul.

Now Father Lacombe was about to move on a more dangerous mission; to the Blackfoot whose fierceness and hatred of the white — including missionaries — was legendary.

Father Lacombe, however, didn't put much stock in legend. Particularly legend about the Blackfoot. Had not their leaders already approached him several times with an invitation to visit their people? And had they not told him that he would need to carry only a white banner emblazoned with a red cross to guarantee his safety throughout their lands?

All that summer he labored among the nomadic tribes. In one sense, his labors were discouraging. Although he made many friends, he made few converts.

Proud and stubborn, the Blackfoot refused to turn from their old beliefs — particularly not to a religion that taught the subservience of man, and that demanded the unthinkable sacrifice of abandoning the harem in favor of life-long devotion to one wife!

It was a depressed Father Lacombe who, on a December night that year, dropped off to sleep in the lodge of the Blackfoot chief Natous.

Pressed by the scarcity of food in their own territory, Natous and other Blackfoot leaders had led their people northward — dangerously close to the dividing line between their territory and that of the Cree.

Late that night, as Natous and Father Lacombe lay

asleep in their thick cocoons of buffalo robe, the Blackfoot camp was suddenly torn by the wild shrieks of war cries and by a hail of Cree bullets and arrows.

Father Lacombe, shocked awake, lay in rigid disbelief as he heard the night echo with the deadly struggle outside.

Most of the Blackfoot warriors were away hunting for game, and it was a pitifully small force that was left to withstand the large force of Cree and Assiniboine bent on slaughtering the camp.

Father Lacombe was jarred to his feet when musket balls tore through the chief's lodge and snapped two of the supporting poles.

Hastily, he threw his black robe over his buckskins, grabbed the cross of his order and his red-cross flag, and rushed outside.

Father Lacombe wasn't afraid. He was enraged. Feeling certain there were some Christians among the Cree attackers, he yelled repeated commands to them to stop their treacherous attack.

Fortunately for Natous and his braves, the echo of the gunshots had carried to the other Blackfoot camps. Hurriedly, hundreds of warriors — the fiercest the west has ever known — were grabbing weapons and leaping on horseback.

The Cree and Assiniboine had already overrun most of the camp, and had begun looting, when the Blackfoot warriors fell on them.

The Cree party retreated, but only to the cover of a nearby hill. Three times that night they mounted fresh attacks on the Blackfoot.

By dawn, both sides were dug in and exchanging a steady hail of musket fire.

With the coming of light, however, Father Lacombe decided it was time to call a halt. Raising his crucifix in one hand and his red-cross flag in the other, he called on the Blackfoot to stop firing.

The Blackfoot complied, then watched astonished as the little priest deliberately marched out into the middle of the battlefield and the rain of Cree musket balls falling through the morning mist.

The Blackfoot could not believe his bravery.

"Here, you Crees!" Father Lacombe yelled at the unseen enemy. "Kamiyo-atchakwe speaks!"

The Cree could not see him in the mist. Nor could they hear his voice over the gunfire.

The Blackfoot, realizing his peril, begged the priest to turn back.

Suddenly, horrified, they watched a musket ball hit the frozen ground and rebound up into Father Lacombe's face. The priest staggered and fell.

The Blackfoot could not know that the ball had only scratched his temple. To them, it seemed that the hated Cree had killed their friend, the powerful white medicine man who had nursed their sick and wounded, and whose bravery seemed a hundred times greater than their own.

An unbelievable anger swept over the Blackfoot, and the warriors leaped to their feet as one, charging past the fallen priest to the heart of the Cree position.

The Cree, suddenly smothered by Blackfoot, broke and ran. For hours, from hill to hill and coulee to coulee, the retreat continued. With every cover, the Cree would turn and fight, only to be forced to run again.

It was during one of these lulls, while the Cree lay in cover, that they heard the scorning yell of a Blackfoot warrior:

"You have killed your blackrobe, dogs! Have you not done enough?"

The message swept through the ranks of the startled Cree. Was it true? Had they really killed their friend, their man of prayer, their honored Kamiyo-atchakwe?

Terrified and ashamed, the Cree and Assiniboine lost all will to fight. What had, up to now, been a retreat became a rout.

A few days later Father Lacombe, wounded and desperately ill, left the Blackfoot for a period of recuperation at Rocky Mountain House.

Despite his physical condition, Father Lacombe left with a strong feeling of satisfaction. He had earned the faith and friendship of the Blackfoot; a faith he was rightly confident would pay off in conversions later. Also he felt — again rightly — that his intervention in the battle had planted the seeds for a negotiated peace between the traditional enemies.

And, to his lasting honor, he left these fierce, proud people of the plains with a second Indian name: Arsouskitsi-rarpi, "The Man-of-the-Good-Heart."

Of all the tributes that would come his way during his long missionary life, this Blackfoot name would always be among those he cherished most.

* * * *

THE MAGIC MCDOUGALLS . . .

Thousands of people a day stream by a small wooden building in the heart of modern Edmonton. Few give it more than a passing glance, and fewer still know the proud story that lies sleeping behind its doors.

The small building, near the intersection of Jasper and First, is McDougall Church — the lasting memorial of Alberta's first white family, and of a father and son team of missionaries who brought peace and civilization to a raw frontier.

No one, except perhaps Father Lacombe, appears more frequently in the pages of our early history than George and John McDougall.

Elsewhere in these books, the reader will meet John playing a personal role in ending the era of the whiskey traders who controlled most of southern Alberta for nearly a decade. He will meet John again as he witnesses the birth of the fort that would grow to be the modern city of Calgary, and he will watch him play a vital part in shaping an Indian treaty to bring lasting peace to Alberta.

When Rev. George McDougall arrived in Edmonton in 1862, a decade after Father Lacombe, he found only a small trading post and a handful of tumble-down shacks. But he found something more as well; a vision of the future.

In the wind, he confided quietly to his wife, he could hear "the sound of that advancing multitude which will soon fill these prairies . . ."

The determined Methodist missionary then set out to prepare the west for that vision.

McDougall's first mission was 70 miles from Edmonton, at Victoria (now Pakan). It took him a year to build it, and it was the summer of 1863 before he could bring his wife to her new home. With her came her two sons, John and David, her daughters Flora and Georgina, and John's wife, Abigail.

For six years, the Victoria mission would be a bustling, happy place as the McDougalls worked ceaselessly to win the trust of Cree and Blackfoot, and to convert them to a new religion. John worked at his father's side in the missionary endeavors, while David chose to follow a career as a trader.

Progress in the mission was rapid. George quickly gained the warm affection and trust of powerful chiefs. Young John wasn't as skilled with words as his father, but he had a keen eye — and some talents that made him the favorite of younger Indians.

It was these younger Indians who gave John his first Indian name — one that meant "the winner". He earned it by proving himself the fastest runner in the west, consistently beating every man, white or Indian, who raced him.

Never one given to modesty, John used to point to a high hill north of the mission and claim: "Over there, I ran down the hill, across the valley and up another hill, faster perhaps than any man ever did — and not because a buffalo was after me, either!"

By the fall of 1869, the McDougalls had every reason to consider their work at Victoria a success. The mission had grown to include a school, and Indians were flocking to Victoria in such great numbers that the Hudson's Bay Company had opened a post by the mission.

Then, a few months later, disaster struck. A smallpox epidemic swept the west, killing thousands of people. All around the mission were camped dying Indians.

All the McDougalls, except George's wife, were infected, and Mrs. McDougall was left to stand by helpless as both her daughters, and John's wife, died of the dreaded illness.

The McDougalls never spoke of their grief, but its depth can be measured even today. Every female descendent of the family has as her second name "Victoria", in remembrance of the unhappy settlement.

By spring, the McDougall men had recovered well enough to try to re-establish the shattered mission. But, though they struggled for a year, persistent flare-ups of smallpox defeated them.

Finally, in 1871, they gave up and returned to Edmonton which, thanks to the quarantine precautions of the Hudson's Bay Company, had escaped the epidemic entirely.

George McDougall built a new house on a hill east of the

Fort, then built the church that now stands in downtown Edmonton. His wife, burying her sorrow, began teaching school to the children of the Hudson's Bay men — no easy task since she spoke English and they Gaelic.

From Edmonton, the sturdy McDougall missionaries, father and son, spread outward. Soon all Alberta felt the influence of their religion, their firm ethics, and their warm concern for their fellow man.

John, more than his father, took eagerly to the rough and tumble of pioneer life. Often dressed in Indian buckskin, he would use his famous speed and, rifle in hand, take off on foot after buffalo and moose.

By 1875, the McDougalls had built a new mission head-quarters at Morley, west of Calgary. In 13 short years, they had gained so much respect that there wasn't an Indian lodge or pioneer cabin that wasn't open to anyone with the McDougall name.

Even the American whiskey traders, whom John and Father Lacombe were working tirelessly to drive out, liked and respected the young Methodist. Alone and unarmed, John was a frequent and welcome visitor at their forts — a venture that would, for most men, have resulted in a quick trip to the graveyard.

Fortunately, for the student of Alberta history, John McDougall turned to writing in his old age. His journals provide a rare and detailed picture of life here during Alberta's first years, and a portrait of this unusual man.

Recently Calgary's Glenbow Foundation found and published the last of John McDougall's journals. Although he died before he could finish it, the slim volume offers some of his most exciting writing.

One chapter in particular is as vivid a picture of frontier life as has ever been painted. And it shares with its readers

John's painful memories of the second great tragedy of the McDougall family: the death of George McDougall.

"It was now December, 1875," McDougall writes, "and in taking stock of our provisions we found the supply was limited. Accordingly my brother David and I arranged to strike out for a buffalo hunt.

"Gathering up our horses we pushed out to the big open country to the east. Our objective point was down into the Rosebud region north-east of where Calgary now lies.

"After scouting in several directions and finding no game, and as the cold was intensifying, we concluded to fall back on our dried provisions and possible cattle at home for another month or two. We were now as a hunting party down to starvation conditions.

"I well remember one very cold evening as we went into camp my brother shot a coyote. When he had taken off the pelt it looked like good meat.

"Our boys and men soon had it cleaned and roasting by our lodge fire. In a little while morsels of this coyote meat, so attractive in appearance, were being passed around. As my share came to me I fully intended to eat it, but in lifting a little of the roast to my mouth I caught its odor and my stomach revolted. I at once concluded to fast awhile longer.

"While we were away on this trip father and mother had gone down to the mouth of Highwood River where my sister Mrs. Wood and her husband were wintering. They planned to spend Christmas with them and also to visit the Blackfeet in that vicinity.

"New Year's eve father returned alone and brought word of buffalo coming up country between the Bow and Red Deer rivers. He had seen them moving westward and he advised me to make a break for meat lest the herds might soon be driven back again by hunters onto the plains.

"The buffalo were still, even as they had been for many years, our main food. To obtain a supply of meat was very essential, for our settlement was growing. In our mission party, permanent and transient, there were all told twenty-three souls. In my brother David's family were five. In the home of the one stockman there were two. In a lodge of French mixed bloods, four.

"On the second of January I began to make ready for a fresh meat hunt. I hired the one mixed blood to go with me and had my young cousin Mose as my third man.

"When ready and about to start, my mixed blood came to tell me that he could not go as his wife was seriously ill. Then my father volunteered to take his place and, while I was most reluctant to agree, there did not seem to be anything else for us to do.

"Behold us then starting out to make the trail and hunt buffalo. Father drove a four horse team hitched to a home-made ironless pair of bob sleighs. Mose and I followed with a string of single-horse flat sleds and the saddle and buffalo-running horses."

(McDougall notes at this point the party was swelled by an Indian friend, Hector Nimrod, and his 10 year old son.)

"We left the valley of the Bow soon after we had crossed the Ghost River, and we struck out into the country north of where the City of Calgary is now located.

"By Friday night we had about half loaded our sleds with meat. This I had done by stalking the buffalo, as there had not been a favourable chance to run them. That night I decided, with father's consent, to fall back west to the last willows as our stock of wood was nearly exhausted.

"Saturday morning we loaded up and travelled some ten or twelve miles back and camped on the bank of a small creek at the foot of a knob of hill which became a first class lookout for us.

"Monday morning we were up and ready for the hunt long before daylight. By sunrise we were near to the spot I had in view, and I had barely time to gather up the horses, give them to father to hold, catch up and saddle one of my runners, when a bunch of buffalo came cantering on towards us. These I tried to run but, as the prairie was frozen hard and glassy and the snow was piled here and there in drifts and also hard on the surface, my unshod horse would not run.

"In vain I tried to spur him on. He very rightly judged that he had enough to do to keep on his feet. However, I picked a good animal and, jumping from the saddle, I made a long, dead shot.

"Straightening out No. 1 in position for skinning, I galloped back to father and put my running pad on another horse and waited for another bunch to appear, which it did shortly. Again I made an attempt to run, but this horse was even more wary of a fall than the first one. Again I sprang from the horse and, making another long shot, brought down my second cow.

"I now made up my mind to take my old war horse Tom out of the shafts and try him once more for a run. Tom had been a famous buffalo horse and was full of pluck. I very soon had my pad on him and, as father and I talked for a few minutes, there appeared another bunch of buffalo over the hill.

"I sent old Tom after them. He, as I hoped, went at his work with all his heart and it was now my turn to feel nervous as, regardless of ice and sharp turn, Tom gathered up speed. Soon we were near the buffalo and I was busy looking for the fat ones.

"I had barely placed a good animal when out from under him went Tom's four feet and down we went, rolling over and over. My gun was thrown one way and Tom in another and my lariat was almost uncoiled to its extreme end before we stopped.

"I was pretty well shaken, but I jumped up and was glad to see old Tom rising to his feet. He seemed to say, 'Hurry, jump on and we'll try again.' Running for my gun and coiling up my lariat, in a moment we were off again.

"Now the situation favoured us, for here was a big dry swamp. The buffalo had eaten off the grass and, in doing so, had left a stiff short stubble which gave Tom firm footing. Soon we were in the herd and I caught sight of four fine farrow cows running in a bunch.

"Tom brought me jump by jump nearer to them and I began to shoot. In a little while the four splendid animals were stretched on the frozen prairie.

"Father and I moved down to my last kill and, beginning at the first, skinned, cut up and loaded it on the sleds. The day was now well spent, and it behooved us to hurry.

"We had finished two and were at the third when I suggested to father that he make a fire with a little bundle of wood we had brought along, melt some snow and make a cup of coffee.

"I well remember that we had five small biscuits. Father insisted that I should eat three of them, while I said I was satisfied with two. Finally, he split the odd one in half and we ate and drank and were greatly refreshed and soon again at work in the dark.

"Just as we were through with the third animal, Hector and his boy came to us with the two sleds and we moved over to the last cow. Hector and I made quick work of this one, and in due time we were ready to start for camp.

"When about two miles from our camp we came to the valley of the west branch of Nose Creek and here, as there was a long incline, Hector, who was leading his horses in front, started into a run.

"With a crack of my whip I sent my four horses after him and thus, for some time, I was parted from father. After we had crossed the creek, pulled up the further bank, and were beginning the long slow ascent up to our lodge, father cantered up.

"He rode to one side and said, 'I will go on, see about Mose, and help him to have supper ready when you come.' Pointing to a bright star ahead he remarked, 'That star is right over our camp John.' I looked and answered 'Yes,' and on into the darkness of the night he rode away.

"I little dreamed that I would never again in this world look upon my living father.

"Presently we were at the dark and silent lodge and I could not imagine what had happened to father as the land marks were extremely good and the night not very stormy.

"I opened the door of the lodge and called, 'Father, Mose; father, Mose,' but there was no answer. In the dark I felt around the inside of the lodge and stumbled over the boy buried under a pile of buffalo robes, sound asleep.

"When he was sufficiently awake to understand, he said he had not seen father. I jumped out and grasped my rifle, which I had fastened on one of the sleds, and fired several shots in rapid succession. I had the Indian shoot off his old flint-lock with heavy charges of powder. Then I said to myself, 'How foolish to make such a fuss. Father may have missed the spot a little, but he will be in before I can get the horses unharnessed. Perhaps he has ridden out to hunt up our horses left here today.'

"With these thoughts I unharnessed the horses and disposed of them for the night. We fired more shots from time to time. We made a beacon light on the summit of the hill, but the long night passed and we still had no clue.

"Hector and I each wore out two horses that next day in riding the country in every direction, but night came and we had not even found a trace. The moving herds of buffalo blotted out other footprints. This condition, with the drifting snow, made it impossible for us to track anyone, experts though we both were at such work.

"We planned to start for home with the early morning. About midnight, however, a wild north-east storm set in and, by morning, thick swirling snow was in full possession of the plains, making it impossible to safely venture out. We waited impatiently for the storm to let up. This did not occur until night again came upon the scene.

"Bright and early Thursday morning we started for Morley. As soon as I got our party over the worst hill and fairly on the road, I left them to come on and hurried home, reaching there late at night. But alas father was not there, nor had anything been heard of him since we had left for the hunt.

"As quickly as we could Friday morning, my brother David, Kenny McKenzie and I started down the Bow valley searching and making all enquiries possible, but without any clue until Saturday morning.

"When near the spot where our hunting lodge had stood, we came upon the track of a horse dragging a long lariat through the snow. We surmised this to be the horse father had with him. Tracking him, we soon came upon him with a little bunch of horses.

"Continuing our search all day, we found ourselves after dark at a native camp. These people had no more tidings for us so we determined to go into Fort Calgary and there obtain all the help possible from the North-West Mounted Police and cover a still wider stretch of country.

"We arrived there through a wild night at one a.m. We roused the police and resident traders, trappers, hunters and arranged for a large search party. Early next day, Sunday, in intense cold, we were away and, spreading out within call of each other, searched all day but in vain.

(The diary records the intensifying search and the final, tragic, result.)

"The following Sunday morning, while searching some brush in a coulee, my cousin Capt. George McDougall who was next to me in line of search, called, 'They are making signs to me over yonder.' I mounted and, as we approached the congregating party, my brother cried, 'Oh John, father is dead. They have found his frozen body.'

"A half-breed who was not with us in the search had, while out hunting buffalo, come upon my father's lifeless body. He had put him on his sleigh and taken him back to his camp and sent us word. The kind native woman had spread her shawl over the lifeless form.

"When I lifted the shawl and saw the position in which he had frozen, I felt whatever may have happened to father toward the last he was conscious and, feeling that death was upon him, he had picked a spot as level as he could and laid himself out, limbs straight and hands folded . . ."

Rev. George McDougall was buried near the mission at Morley. The words with which his son laid him to rest were simple: "His work was finished but will never be forgotten. A faithful son, a true husband, a fond parent, a real patriot, a devoted pioneer missionary. Such was our father."

A visitor to that little wooden building near the busy corner of Jasper and First in Edmonton will find inside old beams hewn with a broad-axe.

Some of the deepest marks in those beams were made by George McDougall. But none of them are as deep as the mark he made on Alberta history.

* * * *

CHARLES MCKILLOP, THE "FIGHTING PARSON" . . .

Southern Alberta in the late 1800's was filled with hard-drinking, hard-fighting cowboys, and any churchman bent on taming this wild flock had to have more than his share of faith and determination.

Charles McKillop arrived in Lethbridge in 1886 with faith and determination aplenty. And with a solid right arm that would leave a lasting impact on many an unruly "heathen".

If Rev. McKillop had any romantic illusions about the task that lay ahead, they were dispelled the moment he stepped off the train in Lethbridge. As he wrote years later:

"No welcoming hand took mine as, tired and travel-stained after a journey of two thousand miles, I stepped out on the platform of the depot. I felt as a stranger in a strange land. I lifted my heart in prayer to my Master to give me courage and wisdom for my work.

"That night, under the pilotage of a Presbyterian whom I had met on the street, I 'roosted' under the roof of what was then known as a hotel.

"The minister's room was one of two directly above the barroom. One layer of inch flooring was all that separated him from the scenes below.

"I went to sleep with the clinking of glasses, bits of ribald song, fierce oaths and a jumble of talk all mingled in my ears. In the middle of the night I was awakened by the sound of a number of shots fired beneath.

"In alarm I jumped out of bed, dressed, and hurried downstairs. The manager, who had heard my moving about, met me on the stairs and said, 'Don't be alarmed, it's only the boys shooting for drinks. Come in and look on!'

"On doing so I found a number of men, seemingly in the best of humour, shooting at cards tacked to the wooden walls of the room. 'Only our western way of doing things,' remarked the manager. 'Not bad fellows, perhaps a bit rough'. . . "

When McKillop left the hotel in the morning, he was met by startled stares and suppressed laughter. Innocent in the ways of the west, the 38-year-old minister was turned out in a very proper black, broadcloth Prince Albert coat, clerical collar and tall silk hat.

As he quickly discovered, it was the fine "topper" that was attracting all the attention. In the west of that time only Indian chiefs wore top hats — and they usually cut holes in the crown for ventilation.

The social error, however, was about to lay the foundation of McKillop's reputation as the "fighting parson" of Alberta.

"While going about my pastoral duties," he recalled later, "I had occasion to pass the window of a certain office . . . I was attracted by a loud tapping on the panes. I stopped, looked back and saw a number of grinning faces behind the glass. On a sudden impulse, I quickly stepped into the office, which was a few feet above the level of the street.

"A young lawyer, who has since become a very notable figure in western politics, and who was evidently ring-leader and spokesman on this occasion, remarked in his drawling manner, 'Mr. McKillop, we merely wished to know where you got that hat?'

" 'Well, gentlemen,' said I, very pleasantly, 'if you will

permit me to put my hat and coat on this shelf, I will give you an answer that perhaps will be satisfactory.'

"Having rid myself of my coat and the obnoxious hat, I turned and faced the half-dozen young men who formed the gang, none of whom seemed formidable, and said, 'Gentlemen, for answer, I propose to pitch you all out of this office.'

"A chorus of jeers greeted this statement. Like a whirl-wind I turned myself loose, as we say in the west, and in a few minutes — the job was done!

"As I stood on the doorstep looking at the sprawling figures, I quietly asked, 'Do you desire any further informa-tion, gentlemen, about that hat?'

"The lawyer, who is a good fellow and a humorist, said, as he was dusting his coat, 'Mr. McKillop, I am very sorry to say that I seem to have lost all interest in that hat.' "

McKillop, the citizens of Lethbridge respectfully noted after that incident, was no ordinary minister.

What he had grasped right from the start was that, on a frontier where might was still right, it was going to take at least a measure of might to bring peace and civilization.

McKillop was uniquely well-suited for the task. He had come to the ministry late in life. In the years before he assumed the clerical collar, he had trained as a boxer and a wrestler — and polished his fighting skills in the rough and dangerous logging camps of northern Ontario and Quebec.

He never lost his interest in hand-to-hand encounter and, two years before his death, the aging McKillop proudly mas-tered Ju-jitsu and was giving free demonstrations to anyone foolhardy enough to take him on.

Only once did Rev. McKillop come close to earnest

combat — and that was the result of a misguided practical joke.

McKillop had been giving instruction in Latin and Greek to a young student in the Methodist ministry who informed his teacher that he understood a new family of Presbyterians had arrived in town and told McKillop where to find them.

The next day McKillop went out to visit the family. Fortunately, before going up to the house, he stopped in next door to visit a parishioner.

He asked the mother of the house if she knew anything about the strangers as he had heard they were Presbyterians.

"Oh, mercy no!" the startled woman replied. "They are dreadful people; you mustn't call there as they'll kill you."

"I'm not in the least afraid," the minister said and, now forewarned, he went next door. The front door of the cottage was ajar and he could hear the sound of hammering inside. McKillop knocked.

The response was a gruff male voice telling him to "Get to hell out of here."

McKillop immediately threw open the door, and stepped inside to see a huge man on knees, nailing down flooring with the back of a broadaxe.

"What do you mean by talking to me like that?" the minister demanded.

The man jeered. "What business have you preachers to come around here when you think that the men-folk are away at their work?"

"None of your vile insinuations, or I'll give you a lesson you will not soon forget." McKillop strode over to the man and commanded; "Put down that axe."

The man put it on the floor and the minister kicked it into the corner.

"Now get up and sit on that chair," he ordered.

Taken aback, the man complied. "You're a pretty likely-looking fellow," he said, staring at the minister.

"I've licked far better men than you," McKillop pointed out grimly. Then he noticed a girl peering at them through the open back door. "Is that your daughter?" he asked.

"Yes, that's Rosie."

McKillop beckoned to the girl. "Come in, Rosie, and sit beside your father, as we're going to have worship."

In minutes, the astounded father and daughter found themselves kneeling in prayer.

When they arose, Rev. McKillop's tone was soft and friendly. Shaking hands with both of them, he invited them to attend church services the following Sunday — which, to the pleasure of the minister, they did.

As the years went by, Rev. McKillop, to his satisfaction found fewer and fewer occasions when he had to display his might. The congregation of Knox Presbyterian Church grew steadily, and Lethbridge nights were no longer interrupted by the sound of gunshots.

But even though he was well into his 50's, the fighting parson had lost none of his keen enjoyment of the wrestling ring.

One morning, not long after he had mastered Ju-jitsu, he was sitting at his front door when Charlie Hyssop, the town's waterman, arrived carrying his huge buckets of water.

Charlie was a giant of a man, well over 250 pounds, and a keen student of wrestling.

Waterman and minister were soon cheerfully debating the merits of a famous wrestler who had died not long before.

"Well," said Charlie, "what do you say to trying out your pet system of wrestling against mine?"

The two, stripped to shirtsleeves, squared off. Before Charlie knew what had happened, he found himself sailing over the minister's shoulder, through the open door, and onto the lawn.

Mystified, the waterman leapt to his feet and jumped back inside. A few seconds later he found himself once again sailing towards the lawn.

Utterly humiliated at being tossed about by an aging man barely half his size, Charlie made good his escape.

The match, however, was to be Charles McKillop's last.

A few months later, he was felled by a stroke and, on August 20, 1907, he died.

There were some, even in his own day, who criticized him for his reputation as the fighting parson. But there were more, many more, who saw him as a man with the right qualities for the temper of a raw frontier.

Charles McKillop was a soldier of the Lord. And he knew, better than most, that sometimes a soldier has to fight . . .

PIONEERS

OF ELEPHANTS AND WEDDINGS . . .

Alberta is, in many ways, still uniquely a frontier. Ask any farmer. Ask any lineman slashing a narrow trail through the trees on the east slope of the Rockies. Ask, for that matter, any city dweller who stops his car on a rural road and steps out to let his eyes search the rimless prairie.

So the title "pioneer" is one that has to be used carefully in this province. And only time will tell if the few people whose stories follow are any more deserving of it than the bearded man in Peace River country carving a homestead out of virgin land and reading this page today by the light of a coal-oil lamp.

* * * *

Looking back into history at our earlier pioneers, the ones we recall best are those who were particularly brave or particularly colorful. Or the ones who had the strangest stories to tell.

One of the most unusual stories has to belong to a man whose name we don't know — and who we can only guess came to Alberta.

The man was a sailor on a British privateer, part of the era before English seamen took on the Spanish armada and won. The man was part of an expedition trading by force in the West Indies when this side of the world still belonged to Spain.

The man, and dozens of his shipmates, became mutinous and were forcibly marooned on the coast of Mexico.

Somehow this sailor managed to walk from Mexico, clear up North America and be rescued off the coast of Canada's maritimes.

*Fragments of the story he carried back to England have survived. He described the Great Lakes to listeners who still thought America was only a sliver of land, separating the Atlantic from the China seas.

Most importantly to us, he described the prairies, and the great hump-shouldered "buffes" running across the grass in thousands.

And he described something else — something plains Indians tried to tell our first white settlers about years later — and left historians with a puzzle they still haven't solved.

This unimaginative seaman described an elephant, long-tusked and covered with shaggy hair, and claimed he'd seen it on the prairies. If he was telling the truth — and if the drawings Indians made years later are to be accepted — the Hairy Mammoth was wandering Alberta a thousand years after the civilized world considered it extinct.

* * * *

Then there was Nigger Molly, the Medicine Hat washer-woman who proudly claimed she was "the first white woman in the west." And there was her arch-rival, Irish-born Slippery Annie.

For years, it was even money which of these two hard-drinking, hard-fighting women would come out the winner in their never-ending battle.

But it was Slippery Annie, finally, who carried the day with as unusual a wedding as the west had seen.

The good Annie found herself a diminutive French-Canadian from Quebec and pointed him towards the church.

The whole town turned out to see Annie in purple dress and fine linen, and her groom-to-be in his frock coat, white vest and silk hat.

Unfortunately, both bride and groom were in an advanced state of inebriation. Once inside the church, Annie commandeered the organ and turned loose with "Pop Goes The Weasel" and "Gin a Body Meet a Body Comin' Through the Rye" and other entertaining — but singularly inappropriate — songs.

The minister tried in vain to bring the concert to a halt. Finally, losing all patience, he ordered Annie out of the church with instructions to come back when she and her beaming boy friend were both sober.

Annie, however, changed his mind with a simple, tearful truth. "The trouble, yer riverence, is he won't come back when he's sober."

* * * *

And there is Billy Henry who, close to a hundred years old, spent one night in an old-folks home then stomped out and went back to his own cabin near High River. He couldn't stand the institution, he told the relatives who finally found him, "because there are too many old people in there."

The stories go on and on. These are the people who haven't just earned a place in our history. These are the people who are our history.

* * * *

THE "SMOKED IRISHMAN" . . .

John Ware was a big man, a solid man.

And he was a dark man.

One summer Saturday in 1970, more than 200 people went to the quiet valley outside Millarville where John Ware built his first home in Alberta. They came to picnic and to laugh and to exchange stories about the Negro cow man who was born into slavery in the southern United States and rose to become one of Alberta's most honored pioneers.

There were old people in the crowd — people who had known John Ware as a neighbor, and who had respected and liked him. And there were youngsters there, playing along the banks of the creek that had once provided the Ware cabin with water.

The four surviving Ware children were on hand. Janet — "Nettie" — to shake her head at the playing children and remember that: "Lord, I don't know as how we didn't drown in that creek a dozen times. We were playing there all the time."

Grey-haired and cheerful, she pointed out, over and over again, the pine tree on the hillside where the cellar of the old Ware cabin used to be.

Her sister, Mildred, huge-eyed and shy, just listened and shook her head at questions. "You'd best ask Nettie. I was too young to remember anything from then."

Bob and Arthur Ware, grey-haired and solemn, circulated through the crowd, exchanging memories with the men and women who had known their father.

Bob Ware frowned when someone asked him why the family had objected, finally, to the "Nigger John" name by which his father was known until a few years ago.

"There were lots of kinds of men who settled this country. Some was Irish and some German and some half-breed Indians.

"I don't remember anybody being called Half-breed Sam or German Joe."

Then he stared, unspeaking, until the embarrassed questioner turned away.

"Anyway," one old-timer commented, "no one would have called him Nigger John to his face, I'll tell you."

John Ware himself had always jokingly called himself a "smoked Irishman". Anyone who dared to make any less flattering reference to his color was in for a thumping from the powerful cowboy. Indeed, on one occasion, John Ware threw a man through a hotel window for making a rude reference to his color.

Lazily, with big rough hands wrapped around homemade sandwiches and cakes, the men chuckled and exchanged stories about John Ware.

One man recalled the time John showed up at the edge of Calgary with a herd of cows he wanted to drive east across the Elbow Bridge. The town fathers refused to let someone clutter up their streets — even if they were mostly mud — with a bunch of dirty steers.

John Ware hadn't argued. He'd just waited until midnight and drove the herd through anyway. By the time the town fathers woke up, the deed was done, and John Ware was politely tipping his hat to them from the far side of the Elbow.

Nettie remembered a night when the Ware cabin got flooded out and her dad had plunged into the stream to rescue his wedding certificate. Then he'd hurried the family up the hill and, in his haste to build them a warming fire, accidentally hit his wife on the head with the back of an axe.

Nettie giggled, then pursed her lips. "A man just has one of those days every so often."

In time, when the picnic had ended, Lt. Governor Grant MacEwan arrived, granddaughter in lap, behind a pair of mules.

Then, to the sound of the creek and the playing children, the lieutenant-governor told the story he has told so often about his favorite pioneer.

About how John Ware was born in slavery. How he couldn't read or write and had no shoes until he was 20. How John Ware signed on, in Texas, with a cattle-drive north and was given the worst horse and the worst saddle and left to ride "drag" — eating dust all the way to Alberta.

About how, when John Ware asked for a better horse, he was given an outlaw — and broke both it and the prejudice against the color of his skin.

Grant MacEwan, like Nettie, pointed to the pine tree on the hill and talked about John Ware building his home and bringing his new bride there.

Then he talked about how John Ware died, too young, 65 years ago when his horse stumbled in a gopher hole and rolled on him.

(At John Ware's funeral, the minister had said: "John Ware was a man with a beautiful skin. Every human skin is as beautiful as the character of the person who wears it. To know John Ware was to know a gentleman, one of God's gentlemen.

"Never again will I see a colored skin as anything but

lovely. He leaves me with the thought that black is a beautiful color — one which the Creator must have held in particularly high favor because He gave it to His most cheerful people.

"Make no mistake about it, black can be beautiful.")

Then the lieutenant-governor found the words the old-timers had been looking for all afternoon.

"John Ware was a good neighbor, and he was a good friend."

The lieutenant-governor stepped over and uncovered the plaque on a rundlestone memorial the Millarville Historical Society had found near Canmore and moved to this spot in memory of John Ware.

Anyone can go and see that memorial any time. It is a big stone and it is a solid stone.

And it is a dark stone.

* * * *

BUFFALO BUD . . .

Time does funny things to a man. It would seem reasonable that anyone who was riding the Alberta range in 1906 would now be content simply to find a warm spot in the sun and sit there.

But E.J. "Bud" Cotton is, well, just plain getting younger and more active all the time.

Which is a very fortunate thing, because Bud Cotton is a pioneer with a rare and valuable set of memories to share. He's one of the last Albertans to know intimately the age of the buffalo.

Actually, the buffalo age he knew wasn't the first — the one that littered the prairie with bleached bones. It was the second age, the one that wouldn't have happened if the fed-

eral government hadn't, at the last possible moment, decided it might be worth saving a few of these mighty animals.

Young Bud Cotton was cowpoking on the Pat Burns
spread when the government opened the Wainwright National Buffalo Reserve in 1909.

Four years later, through some set of events he still can't
comprehend, he turned his back on the Herefords and signed to ride herd on the buffalo; a career he followed until
the reserve was turned into an army base in 1940.

Today, Bud Cotton lives in Calgary where he carves exciting things from wood and from words, and where he is always available to reminisce about a way of life that will never be again:

"You ask, stranger, what it was like when the buffalo ran wild in the big park at Wainwright. Well, there were miles of rolling prairie, clumps of poplar and willow in the low spots and around sloughs, high ridges of sandhills, here and there a bunch of buffalo grazing contentedly, a few elk standing silhouetted against the skyline, and along the side hills and brush patches, a group of deer nervously browsing or nibbling at a juniper.

"It was a great life riding the buffalo range. I'll never forget my first day. It was early in the spring of 1913 that two cow-waddies, Ed and I, first were introduced to the buffalo.

"We had been riding the range in central and southern Alberta. Now we were given the opportunity to ride in the Wainwright Buffalo Reserve. Here was something different, with a promise of unknown excitement — certainly a change from the cow-camp!

"Upon reporting for duty, we were given a couple of saddle horses. We supplied our own saddle gear and bedrolls as was the custom in those days. Then we were told to try and get a count on the buff herd and check for casualties.

"Nine hundred or more buffalo had been turned loose in the reserve — 200-odd square miles of rolling prairie, sand brakes and river coulees. It took a lot of riding to locate and check on the herd of now approximately 2,200 head that had ranged free and unbothered for four years in this large brush-covered terrain.

"We had lots to learn about our new woolly pals. Lucky

for us the saddle horses were good and buffalo-wise. The one I was riding was a big rangy bay named Frost. Ed was atop a slick chestnut gelding called Nick.

"Now buffalo are funny critters and we had to learn the hard way. Here were two well-intentioned cowpokes just wanting to ride around and do a little counting, peaceful-like.

"In cowland tallying, saddle strings were used, tying a knot to represent 50 or 100. But the new boss, apparently with little faith in our cipher education, gave us two punch clocks. We'd squeeze a little gadget for each 'buff' seen, and up popped the totals.

"We drifted towards a bunch of buffalo, and they promptly broke into a run, scattered, and disappeared into the willows and muskeg. Well, no count!

" 'There's some big ones over here,' yelled Ed.

"Twenty head of old bulls for the tally clock! They too drifted into some timber, and to make sure we had 'em all, we moseyed in too. The bronc didn't seem to like this. Suddenly we realized why: One old bull that had been standing, backed up against some brush with his tail straight up, gave a grunt and charged straight at us.

"The wise saddle horse had apparently known just what to expect. Both ponies wheeled and got out of there pronto. I lost my hat as my spine hit that saddle cantle with a tooth-rattling jolt.

"The bull only charged about 40 yards, but oh boy, could he come fast! Again no count — forgot to punch the tally gadget!

"Riding over a knoll we spied quite a little herd grazing along the shores of a small lake. It looked as if our count could really start now. But the unpredictable buffalo fooled us again.

"We had approached them through a ravine that was apparently their chosen way out, and out they came! There seemed to be buffalo everywhere, all travelling fast: so we travelled fast too. No count! And lesson number three: Don't try to figure out which way a buff will run.

"One more try that day sent us back to the bunkhouse disgusted with our luck and in disgrace with our saddle broncs. I could tell it by the way they wagged their ears and shook the bit chains.

"It had happened this way. While we were circling a lovely lake, sandy beach, coves and all, a good place to water the horses and relax awhile, we saw them. There were only a dozen or so of the old buffalo cows and their cute little newborn calves, apparently feeling quite sociable, just standing there looking us over as we rode along the water's edge.

"I noticed the old saddle horse roll his eyes as we passed the closest cow and he acted as if he hated to turn his rump to the old lady. I figured he was just acting gentlemanly.

"Then there was a snort and Mrs. Buffalo charged right in under the bronc's tail, circled back and got set for another run. However, taking the hint, the broncs were out belly-deep in that lake.

"Every time we forced the horses toward the shore, that vengeful old cow would charge us. Cussing did no good, so with the best grace possible two cowpokes went across that lake.

"I told Ed to punch 10 cows and 8 calves on the tally clock, but in the excitement he had lost it in the lake. No count! Four runs — four errors!

"No wonder our broncs took a dim view of us, but despite that I gradually grew to respect and admire those shaggy beasts.

" 'God's critters.' That's the right name for the buffalo. Some folks call them ugly and ungainly brutes, but I always see them as a majestic animal, big and powerful, kings of the North American rangeland.

"In the days when our wild life ran free and unrestricted, they dominated the range. Even the old grizzly bear thought twice and had to be mighty hungry before he tried for a buffalo steak.

"Don't let me throw a scare into you about the buffalo though. They are not vicious. You could ride the buffalo range for weeks and watch them as they roamed there — hundreds of them contentedly grazing or streaming along the old buffalo trails to some waterhole or new pasture.

"It was only when those things on horseback came around trying to corral them and interfere in their way of life that they really got peeved and riled up and certainly made life interesting and miserable for those same pests of buffalo-dom — the riders.

"The buffalo herd bulls generally ranged in bunches of a couple of hundred or so and did not mix with the cow herd. The cows roamed in family groups, just mother, junior, and her two and three year olds, with perhaps a granddaughter or so in the herd.

"June and July is the mating season. The hills and flats resounded to the roaring challenge of the mating bulls. Here nature demonstrates her code of 'the survival of the fittest'. In buffalo land that means 'might is right'.

"The bull fight is really a spectacle of sheer brute strength and tenacity, coupled with the urge to kill. Two tons of infuriated buffalo meet, out for murder, all for the favor of a sloe-eyed buffalo heifer who, by the way, usually calmly wanders off with another gentleman during the fight.

"There are very few preliminaries in the battle. It's a crash-bang, head-on affair with flying dirt and hair as these mighty animals meet with 'no holds barred'. Action is unbelievably fast as each exerts every effort to get a horn into the other's side, groin, or flank, and when this happens it's generally finis — a buffalo doesn't hook. The horn goes in and then, with an upward rolling swing of that mighty head, the horn tears its way through hide and muscle.

"With a ghastly wound like that, especially in the side or groin, it's only a matter of days before the vanquished fighter's carcass is found in some isolated spot where the animal has crawled away and died — alone, with only the magpie's chatter and a coyote's howl as a farewell lullaby.

"Other bulls escape, crippled and soured on life in general, and pass the rest of their days in what we called the 'Outlaw Gang' — confirmed bachelors!

"Nowadays, when all the buffalo are confined to smaller fenced areas, I guess they could all be called imprisoned outlaw gangs of today's civilization, but to me when running free they were 'God's Critters'."

Many a man with Bud Cotton's memories would spend his time brooding about the "good old days." But not Mr. Cotton. Instead, with his carving tools, he carefully recreates in wood the scenes of a past too few are still around to recall.

Maybe that's the secret of growing "young" as a pioneer.

* * * *

THE VOICE OF THE PARK COUNTRY . . .

Red Deer's Annie Gaetz has never much thought of herself as a pioneer. Indeed, she is going to be pretty surprised to find herself singled out as one in these pages.

But then Mrs. Gaetz doesn't even think of herself as an author — despite the success of her book "The Park Country" — so maybe she deserves a few surprises.

Mrs. Gaetz is 90 years old, and her eyesight has failed to the point where she can barely see to peck out a few letters on the keyboard of her typewriter.

But she's an energetic, bustling example of all the strength and determination Alberta's first women brought to a raw frontier.

She was 21, a product of solid United Empire Loyalist stock and a proud Nova Scotian, when fate turned her westward in 1903.

"I had a very bad cough," she recalls. "I went to see the doctor and found out I had tuberculosis. If I would stay home, and do nothing but look after myself, I might live for quite a few years.

"Well, that didn't suit me at all, and I thought that if I was going to die I might just as leave die out here as die there."

Young Annie had been trained as a teacher and she discovered that the prairies — in addition to being a good place for someone with a cough — badly needed teachers.

That combination was enough to make her bundle her belongings together and climb on a train west.

"When I came out, I came on a colonization train. All it had was those slatted wooden seats — not very comfortable, I'll tell you.

"I was on that train six days and six nights, and all it did was stop and start, stop and start. I got so train sick that I just couldn't stand it any longer.

"The next morning I got off the first time we stopped and took off all my things with me. The place was Woolsey and when I saw it I wished I'd had the courage to go to Moose Jaw, which is where my ticket was for. It was just a little place, with only a few buildings and a station.

"I saw there was a hotel right close by, and I went into the station and asked the agent when the hotel would be open. He said, 'It will be open at 8 o'clock, but you don't need to look for a room there because I know there isn't one.'

" 'Well,' I said, 'and where would I get a room?' and he said 'Nowhere that I'd know of.'

"Finally, he told me that a woman across the street kept a boarding-restaurant and her men left at 7:30 to go work on a construction project in the country, and they took their dinners and didn't come back 'til night. 'Perhaps if you ask her, she'd let you rest in one of their rooms.' "

When the woman saw young Annie, worn-out and ill, she let her use her own bedroom to rest. But by 11 that morning, Annie was back up, washed and dressed and heading determinedly for the "Employment Agency" building she'd spotted from the station platform at dawn.

The man inside told her that, yes, he could fix her up with a teaching job — at a place outside a little town called Red Deer.

"I said I'd take the school, and then he told me that they'd said if he got a teacher to keep her there a month, because nobody came in from there but once a month.

"So I said I'd stay if I could find a place to sleep — I didn't know what I'd do otherwise anyway with no train coming or anything.

"I went back to see the woman who'd let me rest in her room, and she said she'd ask everybody she saw if they knew where I might find a room. She tried real hard, and finally she said, 'The only one I can come up with is the girl who works here in the kitchen. She stays with her sister quite close to here, and the sister doesn't really have any room even for her. She only has a kitchen, a bedroom and a small sitting room. But she gives the girl two blankets and a pillow and lets her sleep on the floor.

" 'Anyway, I asked, and they said if you can't find anything else you can go sleep there with her.' "

Annie accepted the offer gratefully and for the next three weeks shared the floor of the crowded house with the young kitchen girl.

Finally word came that a man had arrived from Red Deer — to get a wagon-load of lime and the new teacher.

"We went out on Saturday," Mrs. Gaetz remembers with a smile, "on that wagon-load of lime. It was a double-box wagon. I'd never seen one before. The seat was way up and

I wondered how in the world to get up there, because there was no sidewalk or anything to help you up from the ground.

"And it was just time for the beer rooms to open, and there was a good order of men waiting for their morning refreshments — so I had lots of audience, I'll tell you.

"Anyway, with some help, I managed to get up on that seat, and we were on our way . . ."

Mrs. Gaetz talks without complaint of the year she spent in the one-room school, trying to instill a sense of learning in 31 restless children ranging in age from 5 to 16. She had no textbooks, no notebooks or pencils, no maps, no help. Just a cracked blackboard and some pieces of chalk and a lot of Nova Scotia determination.

Most of those school-hating children grew up to be her friends.

A year after she arrived in Red Deer, Annie married the son of Rev. Leonard Gaetz, one of the founders of the town, and assumed all the arduous chores of a pioneer wife and mother.

Year after long year, she watched the world growing up around her, and she remembered what she saw. One day, a relative suggested she write a little book about the Gaetz family, and she did. Then she wrote another little book and, finally, the big book that is the best history there is of the Red Deer district.

All this and much, much more Annie Gaetz told me one autumn day in the little house, in a quiet corner of Red Deer, where she lives alone.

To say that Annie Gaetz lives alone is somewhat less than the whole truth. She lives with a host of bright memories — memories intertwined in the rich fabric of Alberta's history.   * * * *

RIDERS AND ROPERS

OPEN THE CHUTE . . .

It was 1912, the first year of the Calgary Stampede, and an eastern lady was sitting on a corral fence watching a cowboy saddle and board a bronc.

The woman's brow quickly clouded with indignation. "Oh, look at that pony jump around, and that brute of a man is kicking him in the tummy!" she exclaimed.

Then, as the pony did some real sunfishing, the rider lost his hat, then both stirrups, then was thrown looping over the pony's ears just in time to receive a hoof print "right where mother used to apply the cane."

He rolled to a dusty stop against the corral poles, then slowly picked himself up and gingerly poked all his aching joints to make sure he was still intact.

Satisfied, he ambled over to the still indignant easterner. "Sorry, ma'am," he apologized, "I didn't mean to hurt the little pony. I just had to get off to pick up my hat."

* * * *

It's easy to be a rodeo rider, as easy as falling off a horse — which is probably where the whole thing started.

The sport of rodeo may not have been born in Alberta, but it sure did its growing up here: to a stature unequalled anywhere else in the world.

The basic rodeo skills of riding and roping and wrestling were the natural product of cowboy life. Every working cowhand had to be able to ride a horse that didn't want to be ridden, and able to persuade stubborn cattle to do what he wanted them to do.

The point, of course, was that some men could do these things better than others. And there were others who thought they could do them even better still. And with that attitude around, it was only a matter of time before these skills were pitted in competition.

Indeed, by the time pioneer cowboys were moving into the short-grass country of southern Alberta, it was no longer enough for a man just to be a "good" rider and roper. He had to be an outstanding one.

It was no accident that John Ware, the famous Negro cowboy, first had to "prove" himself by boarding and beating one of the meanest broncos available. And it was no accident that his success was followed in short order by promotion from riding "drag" (in the dusty rear of the herd) to foreman of the Bar-U Cattle Co.

The cowboy competition of rodeo has always been a natural as a spectator sport, with highly-skilled men pitting their talent against the determination of wild and powerful animals.

Thanks to the foresight of a handful of men, and the outstanding ability of Alberta cowboys, Alberta has grown to become the rodeo centre of the world. Of the 26 rodeos authorized by the Canadian Rodeo Cowboys' Association, for example, 18 are staged in this province.

Today, of course, with thousands of dollars in prize money at stake, rodeo is no longer a place for casual cowboy competition. Rather, the men who compete at the Calgary Stampede and other big shows are skilled professionals who make their living by being consistently the best in the world.

But the basic quality of rodeo is still — and always will be — the same as it was the first time a determined cowboy climbed aboard an equally determined bronc.

* * * *

THE GREATEST RIDER IN THE WORLD . . .

Alberta is the unquestioned home of rodeo greats. Year after year, our cowboys and cowgirls bring home the top honors and the championship saddles.

With so many greats, it is easy to understand why today only a few people still remember a little cowboy from Pincher Creek who proved himself the greatest rider in the world and, in a few short minutes long ago, gave the sport of rodeo its greatest glory.

It was Winnipeg in 1913 and the announcement had just been made that Emery La Grandeur had won the title of World's Champion Bronco Rider, with a gold medal and a cash prize of $1,000.

As the crowd clapped and cheered, everyone thought the Winnipeg version of the late Guy Weadick's "Stampede" had come to an end. Only Emery La Grandeur knew different.

"While the announcements regarding winners in other events were being made," Weadick recalled later, "Emery

La Grandeur approached me and asked me if I would do him a favor.

"Sure, I'd be glad to do anything I could for him.

"He then asked me if I would have the big sorrel bucking horse named 'Red Wings' brought into the arena as he wanted to make an exhibition ride on him.

"For my part I had seen about all the bronc riding I cared to during the past week, and told him so, also suggesting that considering he had ridden several top horses during the week — and had been fortunate enough to win the money, title, etc. — it was beyond me why he wanted to prolong the performance fooling around with this 'Red Wings' which, by the way, was an outstanding bucking horse of the Ad Day string.

"Never will I forget the earnestness in his voice nor the almost pleading look in his eyes as he replied, 'Doggone it Guy, don't turn me down in this. I sure want to take a sittin' at that sorrel, and I know the audience will be glad to see one more final bronc ride after the last announcement has been made.'

"Then he continued, 'Go ahead Guy, have them bring him in. You know old Joe La Mar was a friend of mine, and I'd hoped all week that I'd get to draw this Red Wings. Let me take a ride at him, Guy; I want to kinda square things up for old Joe.'

"His eyes sorta filled up as he looked at me — and I, I turned away feeling a little softened up myself. I ordered the sorrel to be brought into the arena at once.

"Emery's eyes sparkled as he heard the order given. 'I'll be right back,' he called over his shoulder. 'Goin' to get my saddle.' "

The attendants brought the big bronc into the arena and snubbed him up to a saddle horse. As Emery was saddling him, an announcement was made that turned the inside of the arena silent as a tomb. The new world champion bronc rider was going to give an exhibition ride on the noted outlaw 'Red Wings' — the horse that had killed the champion's best friend, Joe La Mar, at Calgary the previous year.

In the stands, La Grandeur's wife Violet turned pale and held their infant son a little closer to her.

The area inside the arena fence was cleared, and every man who had competed in the week-long Stampede gathered at vantage points along the rail.

Picking up Guy Weadick's description again: "The saddling finished, La Grandeur climbed up on the bronc, settling himself in the saddle with both feet set in his stirrups. He quietly told the man on the snubbing horse to take the dallies off his saddle horn and pass the halter rope over to him.

"When that had been quickly and quietly accomplished, Emery reached over and unbuckled the halter, stripping it off the horse's head.

"He straightened back up in the saddle and swung the halter in the air — bringing it down between the horse's ears with a resounding crack.

"As the snub man loped out of the way, La Grandeur tossed away both halter and shank and shouted: 'Bow your head bronc, and do your best!'

"Raising both hands high in the air above his head, the reckless rider planted both spurs high in the horse's neck and raked him with both feet from there clear back to the cantleboard of his saddle.

"As the big sorrel plunged forward he really turned on the juice. Not a sound was to be heard from the spectators in the seats nor the contestants encircling the arena, but gradually — it seemed almost unconsciously — all rose to their feet in spell-bound silence; everything forgotten but the drama that was being enacted out there in that long, tan, bark-covered arena.

"Red Wings had a reputation as a top bucking horse, and that August night in 1913 he sure lived up to every bit of it.

"With his big head free and no restraining rein, either to hold him back or to assist the rider in steadying himself, the sorrel really demonstrated that his bucking propensities had not been over-estimated by the many who had touted him as a hard horse to ride.

"He ducked, he plunged, reared, sunfished, leaped high in the air, swapped ends and hit the ground repeatedly like a ton of brick.

"In fact he opened up his entire bag of tricks as he bucked this way and that, zig-zag across and down the long arena.

"The sorrel did everything in his power to unseat the reckless, cool and calculating cowboy astride him — who was still holding both hands high in the air . . .

"And La Grandeur, instead of doing anything to restrain the bucking horse, urged him to still further 'turn it on' by playing a spur tattoo, scratching him continuously high, wide and handsome from shoulders to flanks.

"There was no time limit set to the ride. Nothing had been said as to when the horse was to be picked up, and after Red Wings had bucked the entire length of the arena he swapped ends and started his dizzy waltz back toward the upper end, seemingly getting tougher with every jump.

"Emery still continued to work on him — all the time holding both hands high above his head.

"Suddenly the horse threw up his head and his tail. He broke, and started to run like a race horse.

"The pick-up men immediately started to close in on the fleeing animal and, as there was no halter or halter shank on the horse, they decided to crowd in on him from each side and pick off the daring rider.

"Before these good intentions could be carried out La Grandeur nimbly quit the running horse and landed safely on both feet. The ride was over."

For almost a minute, there was nothing but stunned silence in the arena. Then, suddenly, the crowd went wild. They cheered and shouted in a non-stop tribute to Emery La Grandeur.

La Grandeur struggled through the crowd of contestants trying to congratulate him and made his way to his wife's side.

"You made a fine ride, Emery," she said with a quiet smile.

La Grandeur fumbled in his shirt pocket and pulled out the cheque for the $1,000 prize money and his gold medal.

He handed the cheque to his wife. "Violet, here's the money, it's yours, get what you want with it."

Then he pinned the championship medal on his shirt and commented softly: "It's a purty medal, ain't it?" Violet only nodded.

On the arena floor, one of the top riders in North America, Clay McGonagil of Texas, looked up at the still-cheering crowd.

"All these folks here," he said to a champion, "may live till they're old and greyheaded but they'll never see a bronc ride like that again . . ."

With so many greats, it is easy to understand why today only a few people still remember a little cowboy from Pincher Creek. But it is a little sad, too.

* * * *

THE $100,000 DREAM ...

Around Stampede time in Calgary every year you can find a few sentimentally superstitious cowboys who'll claim they've seen a grey ghost prowling the grounds by dark of night.

It's not a frightening ghost, they'll assure you. Far from it. It's just Guy Weadick back to make sure his dream is still doing well.

The dream of the Calgary Stampede was born in 1908 when the young Wyoming cowboy pulled into Calgary as a performer with the 101 Ranch Show.

Guy Weadick took one look at the bustling frontier city and decided it would be the perfect place to stage the western show to end all western shows — the greatest rodeo and fair in the world.

Weadick managed to infect one of his fellow-performers — a young cowboy named Tom Mix — with the dream, but everyone else around seemed totally immune to Stampede fever.

Everywhere he turned, Weadick found his dream of a show offering unheard-of prize money, a publicity campaign stretching to Mexico, and brand-new facilities, rejected out of hand.

When he approached E. L. (Ernie) Richardson of the Calgary Exhibition, Richardson turned the mad young cowhand down with a flat "No thanks".

Harry McMullen, a former cowman who had taken over the job of general livestock agent for the CPR, was sympathetic to the idea, but he argued that Weadick was "premature" with his dream. Calgary just wasn't ready for the greatest outdoor show in the world.

Discouraged, Weadick left town. A few months later, his prospective partner Tom Mix abandoned the scheme and headed to Hollywood to become the greatest cowboy hero of silent films.

Weadick and his young wife turned to the vaudeville and rodeo circuits with a popular show of tricks and talk — "Wild West Stunts" or "Roping and Gab" or "Weadick and la Due" (Mrs. Weadick's stage name was Flores la Due) depending on where they were playing.

It was three years after his trip to Calgary, in 1911, and

the Weadicks were playing the music halls in England when Guy received a letter from an almost-forgotten Harry McMullen.

The railroad agent's letter was a strong appeal to Weadick to bring his idea back to Calgary again. There was a land boom on and the city was bursting with money and enthusiasm for new ideas.

It was all the encouragement Weadick needed. In early 1912, he was back in Calgary again. On the way, he had stopped in Medicine Hat for a long talk with rancher Ad Day — who assured Weadick he had enough stock "to supply a hundred rodeos" and who hinted that Weadick should try to sell his idea to the "big four" of Alberta ranching: Pat Burns, A. E. Cross, George Lane and A. J. McLean.

Harry McMullen, who Guy looked up as soon as he'd checked into Calgary's Alberta Hotel, shared Day's view that the Big Four were the logical backers of the show.

Weadick decided, however, to have one more try with the managers of the Calgary Exhibition. Again, however, he was turned down flat.

That interview over, Weadick was walking through the lobby of the Alberta when a man stepped forward to intercept him — Alec Fleming, foreman of George Lane's Bar-U Ranch. The message was simple and exciting. George Lane wanted to talk to him about this wild idea he had for the greatest outdoor show on earth.

When Weadick appeared for the interview, he found himself facing not just George Lane, but Pat Burns and A. E. Cross as well.

Weadick's enthusiasm was catchy. Before he knew what had happened the three cattle kings were at the point where they were asking simply how much it was going to cost.

Guy, probably with an eye to dividing things by three,

suggested $60,000. In a matter of minutes he was on his way to the bank with the trio, and listened amazed as they set up a credit of $100,000 for him. Archie McLean, the fourth of the Big Four, had simply been written in as a backer without his knowledge — a fact he accepted coolly when he heard about it.

What the Big Four realized, perhaps better than Weadick himself, was that they'd found the right man with the right idea at the right time.

Their judgment was sound. As it turned out Weadick did so well on advance ticket sales that he apparently never had to touch a cent of the $100,000 credit.

The name Weadick picked for the show was "Stampede"; chosen because it had never been used before, and because of its descriptive and publicity powers.

Weadick's only instruction from his backers was to make the show "the greatest thing of its kind in the world," and he set out to follow it.

The Stampede was scheduled for the week of Sept. 2. At Weadick's instructions, Victoria Park was invaded by carpenters who constructed thousands of bleacher seats. Weadick, meanwhile, was busy recruiting riders and ropers from all over North America and building a publicity campaign to drag in visitors from thousands of miles away.

As Stampede time drew near, excitement in Calgary built to fever pitch. The city fathers suddenly realized that even if all the 40,000 people to fill the new seats in Victoria Park didn't show up, there were still going to be more visitors in town than could be handled.

With the show still more than two weeks away, The Calgary Herald reported:

"Mayor (John W.) Mitchell has sent all over the Dominion asking about tents in which to accommodate the

Stampede crowd next month. He is now receiving wires and letters and expects to secure all he wants.

"It is proposed to make the tent city across the Elbow on the property which the Great Northern bought from Dr. Lindsay. It will be fitted up specially and those who secure accommodation there will be just as comfortable as they would be in hotels."

At the same time, The Herald noted an undesirable, if inevitable, result of the Weadick publicity campaign:

"Warnings from an under-ground source which convey to the police inside information have been sounded. Reports from 2,000 miles away have reached Chief Cuddy regarding the advent of dangerous crooks who are coming for the Stampede. From all over Canada and the northern States talented pick-pockets and confidence men are planning a sortie.

"The chief has been warned in time. When the Stampede opens half a dozen of the most astute sleuths in the employ of the Pinkerton Detective Bureau will be in Calgary to assist the local detectives in rounding up the bad men."

Not all press reports were so ominous. A few days later Harry McMullen, who Weadick had recruited to help manage the Stampede, was quoted in The Herald as saying: *"The pageant on opening day will be the biggest that was ever seen in Canada.*

"There are now in the city waiting for the competitions, cowboys and cowgirls from Texas, Colorado, Utah, Montana, Idaho, New Mexico, Washington and Oregon."

Then, on Aug. 31, The Herald reported that: *"One special train to the Calgary Stampede left Spokane today and a second will follow Sept. 2. The first started from Cheyenne and the second will be made up at Pendleton.*

"By Monday the heart of Calgary will be a blaze of bril-

liant colors, and when His Royal Highness, the Duke of Connaught, arrives the city will be in the vortex of the greatest celebration that has ever taken place in the West."

To open the Stampede, Weadick had hit upon the idea of a massive parade. And when that parade moved onto the streets of Calgary Sept. 2, Weadick had immediate confirmation of the soundness of his dream.

In Calgary, a city with a population of 61,450, an estimated 75,000 people were packed along the parade route.

Mindful of his directive to create "the greatest thing of its kind in the world," Weadick had spent months of careful negotiation with every Indian tribe in Alberta. Those negotiations paid off in the parade as more than 2,000 painted and feathered Indians rode the streets of the city.

Moved almost to literary frenzy, a Herald reporter wrote of *"the wonder of the spectacle of 2,000 western Indians, smeared with paint and decked in the attire of ante-civilized years, who passed through the streets of Calgary yesterday morning.*

"Authentic and seasoned opinions would have it that, never in all the world, since the red men became dominated instead of a dominant influence, has there been such a gathering of the picturesque aborigines who, a few short years ago, roamed these western foothills, unmolested by the white man.

"Verily, it was a spectacle that money could not present. Mayhap, never again will those who watched yesterday's procession have a similar opportunity afforded them."

When the parade was over, a crowd of more than 50,000 crushed into Victoria Park. Once he'd got them that far, Weadick could relax a little and leave the rest to the talent in the show. And what talent it was!

The first of the two special trains from the United States had brought in George Drumheller of the big Drumheller Ranch in Washington and 15 of his best riders — including 1910 world champion Bert Kelly.

Already on hand were virtually every top rider on the continent. There was Joe Gardner of Texas, Ed Echols of Arizona, George Weir from New Mexico, Tex Macleod from San Antonio, Harry Webb from Wyoming, Art Acord of Portland, Otto Kline of Montana, Charlie Tipton from Denver, 'Doc' Pardee and O.K. Lawrence from Oklahoma. There was also a large Mexican contingent headed by Senor Estevan Clemento.

Among the female competitors was the good Mrs. Weadick — registered under her professional name of Florence la Due — who was destined to win the trick and fancy roping crown.

In all, there were 150 competitors.

Ad Day, true to the promise he'd made to Guy Weadick in Medicine Hat months earlier, was on hand and determined to make the competitors work for their prize money. Ready to go into the chutes was the biggest herd of outlaws — from wild and rangey Texas long-horns to top bucking broncs — ever assembled in Canda. And to try the stuff of champions, Day had waiting the greatest bucking horse in the world; that jet-black terror called "Cyclone."

If Guy Weadick thought he had it made at the end of that first day, he learned differently the next morning when he woke up to meet the demon that has plagued so many Stampedes — bad weather.

Rain was falling in sheets, and so was attendance, as riders struggled in an infield that was a sea of mud. Wednesday, the third day of Stampede, was no better. Nor was Thursday when the Royal party arrived.

Also adding to Weadick's worries was the fact that Calgary's hotel and dining facilities just weren't up to the crowd.

Like many others, Weadick had seen the article in Tuesday's Herald noting: *"It is estimated that up to 20,000 visitors are already in Calgary. Yesterday was the busiest day that restaurants and hotels have ever had.*

"From 6 until 9 o'clock last night it was impossible to get into a restaurant and at 9 o'clock many of the waiting hundreds were saddened when the proprietors opened their doors and announced that every digestible had been consumed."

Nevertheless, the show went on.

Thursday, when the Duke of Connaught and Princess Patricia arrived, the Royal party had hardly settled in its box before the rain poured down again.

Weadick quickly decided to move the show into the Victoria Park arena, and soon thousands of people were inside, scrambling for seats.

Watching the show, the Duke was so delighted he decided to make an unscheduled return to the grounds the next day.

The decision seemed to mark a turning point for the show. By Friday morning, the rain had stopped and the crowd was swelling again.

By the time the Stampede ended, Weadick could justifiably claim it had been a success.

Thanks to bad weather and inadequate facilities, however, it wasn't an unqualified success.

In 1913, even though the show had made money, Calgary was unreceptive and Weadick had to take his Stampede to Winnipeg.

Then the war years came and put an end to any such shows in Canada. Weadick made one try to stage the Stampede in the United States in 1916, but it was a financial flop.

It wasn't until 1919, again with the backing of the Big Four, that Weadick and the Stampede returned to Calgary. That year the weather co-operated and the so-called "Victory" Stampede was an enormous success. Finally, in 1923, the Calgary Exhibition had a long-awaited change of heart about Weadick's show, and the amalgamation that followed made the Stampede a permanent part of the Calgary scene.

Weadick was the Stampede's master-mind until he retired as arena director in 1932.

In 1952, he was on hand to present the prizes to the victors in the 40th Calgary Stampede.

Then, the following year, Guy Weadick's career came to an end as a riderless horse, boots reversed in stirrups, led his body to a cemetery.

At least, it seemed to end. It remains a little hard to

account for the grey ghost that wanders the Stampede grounds, smiling contentedly at a dream that came true . . .

* * * *

TAMING THE CYCLONE . . .

The first Calgary Stampede in 1912 was seven days of thrills and spills — with most of the thrills and spills being provided by a snorting, spinning, wild-eyed bundle of black dynamite called "Cyclone".

Cyclone had come to the Stampede as the best bucking horse in the world, and as the show moved into its final day, his record was intact. A total of 129 men had tried to mount him and stay on him, and 129 men had ended up in the dust.

The only man in the world anyone rated as having a chance to beat Cyclone was a young Indian cowboy from Macleod, Tom Three Persons.

But as that closing Saturday dawned, Tom Three Persons wasn't available to take on the horse. Tom, lamenting his fate, was under lock and key in the Calgary jail, and staring vainly through the bars at the distant Stampede grounds.

In Victoria Park, the finals in the bucking horse contest were about to begin, and Cyclone's record of 129 to 0 was about to permit him to withdraw from the competition the undisputed champion.

But an Indian agent named Glen Campbell wouldn't hear of it. Red-faced with anger, he kept insisting that Tom Three Persons should be given a chance at the beast.

Somehow, word got to the Mounties, and they evidently agreed that a little thing like a jail sentence shouldn't keep an Alberta cowboy from showing a crowd how to ride.

With the finals already underway, a cash bond was posted and Tom Three Persons was rushed to the grounds.

A surprised crowd cheered when the announcer gave the word that Tom Three Persons of Macleod was about to ride in the finals. But the cheers gave way to apprehensive groans when the announcer added that Tom would be climbing on the back of Cyclone. Even the other competitors looked sympathetic.

Indeed, the only person who didn't seem worried about it all was Tom himself. As The Calgary Herald recorded the scene:

"The horse thrown to the ground, Tom jumped across him, placed his feet in the stirrups, and with a wild 'whoop' the black demon was up and away with the Indian rider.

"Bucking, twisting, swapping ends and resorting to every artifice of the outlaw, Cyclone swept across the field. The Indian was jarred from one side of the saddle to the other, but as the crowd cheered themselves hoarse he settled every time into the saddle and waited for the next lurch or twist.

"His bucking unable to dislodge the redskin, Cyclone stood at rest and reared straight up. Once it looked as though Tom was to follow the fate of his predecessors. He recovered rapidly and from that time forward Cyclone bucked till he was tired. The Indian had mastered him.

"The thousands created a pandemonium of applause that was not equalled all week. The Princess Patricia and the Duke (of Connaught), who were in the Royal box, leaned far out over the railing, laughing and applauding at the Indians in the enclosure to the north.

"It was a thrilling moment and in it Tom Three Persons had captured the championship of the world for himself and for Canada."

Even though Tom had to return to jail for a while, he emerged as the pride of Alberta's Indians — the only Indian to win the bronc riding championship of the world. Even today, more than half a century later, his picture hangs in the Blood reserve community hall at Standoff; a permanent tribute to a man who walked out of a jail cell to tame a Cyclone.

LAW MAKERS & BREAKERS

OF LAW AND JUSTICE . . .

The temptation to think of Alberta as part of the "wild west" is strong. Indeed, over the years, many story-tellers and — yes — even responsible journalists have given into the temptation.

It's a puzzling business, because the ingredients for these "wild west" stories are just plain missing.

"Oh, it's true enough that Alberta had its share of murderers and rustlers and rum-runners and con men. But it never had them in the legend-inspiring quantity we've been led to believe.

The simple, unromantic truth is that all the gunslingers and organized gangs belong to another part of the west — the part just across that thin line of cairns and steel posts that marks the boundary between Canada and the United States.

Even the young man named Harry Longbaugh spent his time in Alberta busting broncs, and made it a point to go back to Montana before he started work on building his reputation as the Sundance Kid.

This doesn't mean that the story of law-enforcement in Alberta isn't an exciting one. It is exciting — in many ways more exciting than the story south of the border — because, thanks to a laconic half-breed and a pitifully small number of red-coated men, the word "law" in Alberta has always meant the same as the word "justice."

The mating of those two words is one of the proudest events of Alberta's heritage.

* * * *

WHISKEY & WOLFERS . . .

The laws of the Young Dominion of Canada always did apply to the territory that was to become Alberta. The only problem was that there was no one around to enforce those laws, so a lot of people just calmly broke them.

Right into the 1860's, the years of Confederation, the territory was open prey to any brute or opportunist who felt like moving in.

The business of flaunting the law reached its peak in the late 1860's when American traders poured into southern Alberta to use rot-gut whiskey to part Indians from fur and buffalo hides. And when cold-blooded "wolfers" all but took over the plains in search of bounty; poisoning wolves and Indians with equal unconcern.

It was one of these unnamed wolfers who committed the most horrible crime in Alberta history. Enraged by the death of a partner in a fight with some Indians, he went south into the United States, to a town hit by a smallpox epidemic, and brought back hundreds of infected blankets wrapped in oilcloth bundles.

Carefully, he scattered the bundles across the plains of southern Alberta. As he anticipated, the Indians found the bundles, broke them open, and took the blankets back to their camps.

In exchange for his partner, the wolfer collected the lives of thousands of innocent Indians — and went unpunished.

But when another group of wolfers rode into the Cypress Hills and coldly slaughtered a band of helpless Indians a few years later, they enraged a nation, forced the birth of the North West Mounted Police, and rid the southern plains of wolfers and whiskey-traders forever.

* * * *

THE BOW-LEGGED SCOUT . . .

In the fall of 1874, the first small, exhausted force of mounted police was limping into Alberta.

No one could have cared less about that force — or about southern Alberta for that matter — than Jerry Potts.

Jerry Potts, sitting in Fort Benton, Montana, had already had his fill of whiskey traders and wolfers. For the past five years, he had worked as a hunter, providing food for virtually every one of the infamous whiskey forts north of the line.

Fed up with the excesses of the traders and sick of the depredations visited upon the Indians, he had gone south and taken a job for the respectable I. G. Baker and Company.

But, unknown to Potts, two tattered mounties were already riding south to Benton to find him and coax him into a place in Alberta history.

There probably wasn't a man in the west better-qualified for western glory than Jerry Potts.

Potts was born in 1840, the son of a Scot father and a Blood Indian mother. The year Jerry was born, his father was killed by an Indian who had mistaken him for someone else.

Fatherless, Potts was raised for the early part of his life by Alexander Harvey, one of the most notorious and vicious traders on the upper Missouri. By the time he was five, young Jerry knew intimately the pattern of villainy and cunning he would encounter later. This knowledge would, on many occasions, save his life.

When Harvey fled the Missouri to escape assassination by some of his fellow-traders, Jerry was adopted by Andrew Dawson, a gentle Scot, who taught him to speak English, to be a clever fur-trader and — most importantly — to be a just and honorable man.

The mixture of the legacies left him by his two foster-fathers and by his mother would set him apart for the rest of his life.

By the time he was in his late teens, Jerry had taken on the mannerisms of the frontier. Drifting back and forth between the white world and the lodges of his mother's tribe, he developed a passion for whiskey, a way of dressing that was white from the waist up and Indian from there down, and a code of justice as fairly divided between white and Indian as his clothes.

Jerry Potts killed his first man when he was 23, forced to shoot in self-defence during a quarrel with a drunken trader named Antoine Primeau. It was his first, and only, battle with a white.

Potts' warrior skills, when combined with his passion for drinking, sometimes led him into strange escapades.

One old-timer recalls how Potts and a half-breed friend named George Star used to get thoroughly drunk then stand 25 feet apart and try to trim one another's moustache with bullets from their six-shooters. Somehow, although they performed the trick dozens of times, both survived.

So it was Jerry Potts, now 34 and the veteran of Indian wars and whiskey posts, whom the mounties looked up as soon as they got to Fort Benton.

The situation the two red-coated officers outlined to the reluctant Potts was desperate.

The force of 150 men was stranded in southern Alberta. Their guides were unreliable, food was running out, their horses were dead or dying, and winter was only a few weeks away.

Potts listened and pondered. Then, with a grunt he accepted the position of police scout to the North West Mounted Police at a wage of $90 a month.

For that salary, he undertook to guide, interpret, advise — and generally nurse the new force to maturity.

Although he didn't realize it at the time, he had also undertaken a job he would keep to the end of his life.

The two grateful mounties led Potts north that same day to begin his new job. To see how he tackled it, we turn to, Jerry Potts, Plainsman, an excellent booklet by Hugh Dempsey of the Glenbow Foundation.

"His first assignment," Mr. Dempsey records, "was to lead the Mounted Police to Fort Whoop-Up to attack the American whiskey traders. Potts tried to explain that the traders had fled to Montana but, not trusting their new guide, the police forced their crippled horses and tired men on towards the fort. Under the able guidance of the little mixed blood, they travelled across the short grass country from Milk River Ridge, passing buffalo bones bleached in the sun and huge herds of the shaggy beasts grazing like domestic cattle.

" 'He won the confidence of all ranks the first day out.' recalled Sam Steele (one of the party of police), 'and when morning came he rode boldly in front of the advance guard. It was noon when the party reached Milk River and found him there sitting near a fat buffalo cow which he had killed and dressed for the use of the force. To those new to such life he appeared to know everything.'

"It was during this trek that the Mounted Police noticed their guide did not waste words. When they found the riddled body of a dead Assiniboine Jerry was asked to explain the probable reason of the killing. 'Drunk,' he muttered.

"After burying the body, the police continued the journey over the monotonous terrain. Finally, one officer of the force, hoping that Whoop-Up was only a short distance away, rode up to Potts and asked: 'What do you think we'll find on the other side of this hill, Jerry?'

" 'Nudder hill,' replied the laconic guide.

"When they reached Fort Whoop-Up, the Mounted Police found they did not need their two nine-pounder field guns and two mortars. With the exception of an old trader the fort was deserted.

"It was then early October and Col. Macleod, seeing the need for immediate quarters, urged Potts to lead them to a suitable site for a fort. Guiding the tired caravan of redcoats, winded horses, Red River carts and wagons across the rolling prairies, the scout followed an Indian trail westward until they arrived at a large island on the Oldman River. Here was a site that offered natural water protection, abundant cottonwoods for construction, and was on a well-travelled route.

"While Fort Macleod was being built, Potts travelled among the Blackfoot of the area, explaining the presence of the red-coated strangers and gaining promises of non-violence. Late in October, he reported that whiskey was being sold at Pine Coulee and guided the police to the illicit post where the five men were apprehended. This was the first successful raid by the force since arriving in Blackfoot country."

Mr. Dempsey records a trip early in 1875 in which Potts displayed his remarkable sense of direction.

"The trip occurred in March when Col. Macleod, three policemen, and Potts started for Helena, Montana, three hundred miles away.

"When well out on the plains a wild blizzard struck, forcing the men to camp beside a cutbank for two days. When the food and fuel supplies were exhausted, Potts suggested travelling thirty miles south to Rocky Springs where proper shelter was available. Onto the plains of swirling snow the men followed their guide and, within an hour, everyone but Potts had lost his sense of direction. There were no landmarks and weakened men and horses stumbled in exhaustion.

"Finally, after several hours Potts dismounted and led the men into a narrow protected valley. It was Rocky Springs. Later, when everyone was settled before a roaring fire, the police were dismayed to learn that Potts had been almost completely snow blind during the final part of the journey."

In those first six months, Jerry Potts had made himself a legendary figure to the force. It was a legend that would continue to grow and expand for the next 25 years — and that would let Jerry Potts get away with behavior that no one else among the strictly-disciplined mounties would even dream of.

On one occasion, a group of starving Indians appeared at Fort Macleod and their chief treated the police to a long and urgent speech — of which Col. Macleod couldn't understand a word. Potts was called upon to translate, and the long speech was boiled down to three short words: "He wants grub!"

Another time, several Blackfoot chiefs appeared before the colonel and made a round of speeches. Potts, looking magnificently bored, followed his usual habit as an interpreter: he didn't say a word.

Macleod caught one or two words he thought he recognized. "Napi-okee" or whiskey. "Napi-kwan" for white man. He surmised that the chiefs were expressing their gratitude to the mounties for riding the plains of the whiskey traders.

He turned to Potts for his translation and the little guide just shrugged his shoulders.

"Dey damn glad you're here," he assured his colonel.

Even more troublesome to the mounties than his failings as an interpreter was Potts' appetite for whiskey. He would drink anything — from first-class alcohol to rot-gut trade whiskey with equal enthusiasm.

Sometimes Potts had to be tied up until he slept off a violent drunk. Once he almost shot a mountie when he mistook him for an old enemy.

One policeman recalled that the scout had "an unquenchable thirst which a camel might have envied."

Hugh Dempsey records one occasion when Jerry Potts' drinking habits sorely tried the loyalty of his mountie employers. Word had been received that a suspicious wagon had crossed the border from Montana.

"The scout and two constables were sent to investigate the nocturnal traveller and intercepted the wagon after a day's ride. The owners had goods and whiskey in their load so they were arrested and handcuffed together in the back of the wagon.

"One constable took the reins, the other took charge of

the saddle horses, and Potts was placed in the back to guard the prisoners.

"Upon arriving at Fort Macleod a constable discovered that Potts had broken into the whiskey supply and the three men had drunk themselves into an unconscious stupor. The liquor was consumed and the evidence was gone."

Despite incidents like this, Potts never lost the respect of the mounties. Drinking, after all, was a common fault among the men who braved the rough frontier of the west and, in the case of Jerry Potts, the fault was more than offset by his honesty, courage and devotion to the force.

Right to the end of his life, Jerry Potts went on doing the job he undertook that October afternoon in Fort Benton — and doing it well.

Time and again, in his later years, the officers of the Mounted Police would pay tribute to his skill, his faithfulness to the force, and to the diplomatic talent that bonded Indian and mountie in friendship.

When, on July 14, 1896, Jerry Potts died, the Fort Macleod Gazette summed up the feelings of all who knew him:

"Jerry Potts is dead. Through the whole North West, in many parts of eastern Canada, and in England itself, this announcement will excite sorrow, in many cases sympathy, and in all, interest.

"His memory will long be green in the hearts of those who knew him best, and 'faithful and true' is the character he leaves behind him — the best monument of a valuable life."

* * * *

"COMPETENT HORSEMEN OF SOUND CONSTITUTION" . . .

On a warm May 23rd in 1873, word finally reached Ottawa of the infamous Cypress Hills massacre. The reports were wildly exaggerated, but they were all that was needed to sweep Parliament into a frenzy of legislative action.

Before the day was over, His Excellency the Earl of Dufferin, Governor-General of Canada, had given Royal Assent to the bill that brought the North West Mounted Police into existence.

The new force specified by Parliament was to be a semi-military body, the immediate objectives of it being: to stop the liquor traffic among the Indians, to gain the Indians' respect and confidence, to break the Indians of their old practices by tact and patience, to collect customs dues, and to perform all duties such as a police force might be expected to carry out.

As for members of the force, only competent horsemen of sound constitution, good character, and between the ages of 18 and 40, were to be enlisted. All had to be able to read and write either French or English. The command was to be divided into troops. The commanding officer was to hold the title of "Commissioner". Service was to be for at least three years.

Parliament set the size of the force at 300 men. But it was decided, for the time being, to form only three troops of 50 men each.

These men, at the advice of those with experience in the west, were to be clad in red tunics. Blue, the color first considered, would be associated by the Indians with the uniforms of the United States cavalry — a force the Indians hated with a passion that would appear later at a place called Little Big Horn.

By fall, the 150 green recruits had expanded to a force of 300. A year later, exhausted, starving, and with their red uniforms in faded tatters, they finally rode onto the plains of southern Alberta.

In all, 274 men — including guides and drovers — had reached their destination, and began the staggering task of policing 300,000 miles of virgin territory, peopled with a handful of whites and more than 30,000 potentially-savage Indians.

In truth, the commanders of the new force had never really wanted to pit their green troops in open battle against the cunning and dangerous plainsmen of the whiskey forts and wolfer parties.

So, through missionaries and friendly Indians — and through co-operative members of the International Boundary Commission then marking the 49th parallel — the traders and wolfers were barraged with fearsome rumors.

Although the Americans scoffed in public, in private they became increasingly disturbed by the conviction that what was on the way was a hardened army, bristling with cannon and gatling gun.

As the force drew nearer and nearer, the invaders, one by one, then by the dozen, and finally en mass, fled back across the Montana border.

The mounties had won their first battle without firing a shot. When they rode up to the gates of Fort Whoop-Up (which the whiskey men had turned into a fortress they'd sworn to defend to the death), the gates were opened to them by a friendly Dave Akers, the only occupant of the Fort.

The way in which the problem of the wolfers and whiskey men was "solved" was probably the most important single factor in the success of the NWMP in Alberta.

The Indians were awe-struck. None — not even the

proud Blackfoot — wanted to do battle with these mighty men in red who had rid the west of the invaders without firing a shot.

Gradually, as the mounties began to work among them, the Indian feeling of awe was replaced with respect for the fairness with which the redcoats dispensed justice and help to Indian and white alike.

Time and again, in the years to come, that respect would save the west.

* * * *

SITTING BULL & THE STUBBORN MAJOR . . .
Within months of arriving on the plains, the mounties had the business of law and order in Alberta effectively under control.

Everywhere, from one end of the territory to the other, Indian and settler could see the red-coated rider — usually alone — who meant that the peace was being kept.

It was one of these redcoats, face wind-burned and pill-box hat askew, who directed the main body of Mormon settlers to their destination of Cardston.

And it was another, a canny, stubborn major named J. M. Walsh, who calmly controlled the frontier's biggest crisis.

Two years after the NWMP entered Alberta it was still only 250 strong. But it had spread its slim resources carefully and — in the case of the 75-man detachment at Fort Walsh in the Cypress Hills — luckily.

On Sunday, June 25, 1876, at a spot on the Wyoming-Montana border called Little Big Horn, 2,000 Sioux under Chief Sitting Bull wiped out a force of 250 cavalrymen.

Within weeks, with the U.S. army snapping at their heels, the entire Sioux nation — nearly 6,000-strong — was fleeing north across the Canadian border and into the waiting arms of James Morrow Walsh of the North West Mounted Police.

In two years in the west, respect for the fairness of the NWMP had spread to Indians on both sides of the border. Sitting Bull was counting on this fairness, and on the strength of the force he had at his back, for protection from the pursuing American forces.

As soon as Sitting Bull's tribes had made camp around Fort Walsh, the old chief discovered he would get fairness all right — but on James Morrow Walsh's terms, not his.

Walsh, on that particular day, saw his tiny garrison surrounded by thousands of Sioux still flushed and cocky with their bloody triumph over the cavalry, and knew that it was up to him to quiet them down in a hurry.

Never a cautious man, Walsh slapped his braided cap on his head, grabbed a sergeant, three constables and two scouts, and galloped off to find Sitting Bull.

Right in the middle of the Sioux camp, with his tiny escort doing their best not to look nervous, Walsh stuck his jaw out and informed Sitting Bull point blank that he would have to behave himself in Canada and would only be tolerated here as long as he remained peaceful.

It was a remarkable bit of bluster for a man who couldn't have mustered many more than 200 troops in all Alberta, but it worked.

Sitting Bull quietly agreed to all the conditions the redcoat imposed.

So impressed was the chief by Walsh's courage in this first meeting that only once in the four years the Sioux remained in Canada did Sitting Bull try Walsh's patience.

The Sioux were hungry and restless, their warriors spoiling for a fight, and Sitting Bull and a force of his braves rode into Fort Walsh. Sitting Bull was shouting unreasonable and threatening demands when Walsh stormed out of his quarters and across the parade ground.

Jabbing his finger at the astonished chief, Walsh grimly reminded him that he was not a Canadian Indian and Canada owed him nothing but hospitality — and only as much of that as the Sioux were prepared to earn.

And furthermore, he continued, if Sitting Bull and his braves did not behave and stop stealing horses he, Walsh, would arrest them and personally place Sitting Bull himself in irons.

It was a much subdued Sitting Bull who led his warriors back to camp again.

Walsh, fortunately for the west, was much more than a courageous man. He was a skilled diplomat, and it was he, finally, who negotiated the agreement that returned Sitting Bull and his people to the United States.

Walsh was unknown before those four years, and dropped out of historical sight soon after they were over. But those years were long enough to earn him his place as one of the greatest heroes of the plains.

* * * *

CROWFOOT, KEEPER OF THE PEACE . . .

"It was at this time that Crowfoot, head chief of the Blackfoot, paid us a visit. He was full of questions regarding the future. I took time to explain to him the history of Canada's dealing with its Indian peoples thus far and assured him that I expected in due time treaties would be made and a settled condition created in this country wherein justice would be given to all concerned.

"The chief expressed himself as delighted with what I had told him and said that he was much pleased with the change that the coming of the Mounted Police had brought in all the west. He also told me that he would depend upon

me to inform him of anything in the future that would be of interest to him and his people.

"When Crowfoot left me that August day of 1875 I felt encouraged and was thankful . . ." (from the journal of Rev. John McDougall).

All the efforts of the North West Mounted Police, and all the skill of the missionaries and of Jerry Potts, would have come to nothing had it not been for a great man named Crowfoot.

Time and time again, this man who was undisputed leader of the fiercest Indian tribe in the west, and spokesman for the strongest alliance in the Indian nation, single-handedly kept peace in the west.

In 1876, only a year after the conversation recorded in John McDougall's diary, the Blackfoot leader's loyalty to the new order was put to the test.

To Crowfoot's camp in southern Alberta came emissaries of the Sioux, begging the Blackfoot to join them in a daring undertaking.

In the south, the mighty Sioux nation was gathering under Sitting Bull, preparing for final battle with the white man. If the Blackfoot would join the war, it could easily be won.

Join us, the emissaries said, share in the booty, then we will all sweep northward, wipe out the redcoats and settlers, and be rid of the white man forever.

Many of the lesser Blackfoot chiefs were excited and eager to join the Sioux. But Crowfoot stood firm. He spurned the offer, and when it was made again and again, he spurned it again and again; firmly avowing allegiance to the "Great White Mother".

Finally, angry, the Sioux threatened to invade the Blackfoot country. Crowfoot remained adamant, and the Sioux gave up and went home.

In time, Col. Macleod of the NWMP heard of the incident. The relief he felt at Crowfoot's stand was overwhelming. Better than most, he realized how great the power of a Sioux-Blackfoot alliance would have been, and how deadly to the whites.

Macleod sent a message to the chief, promising that if the Sioux attacked the Blackfoot, the Mounted Police would come to Crowfoot's aid.

Then Macleod sent another message, this one to the east, and in time Crowfoot received a letter of gratitude from the "Great White Mother", Her Majesty Queen Victoria.

Again and again, in the months and years that followed, Crowfoot came to the forefront in efforts to keep peace between Indian and white. He even led efforts to negotiate peace with the Blackfoot's traditional and hated enemy, the Cree.

In 1885, Crowfoot's strength and loyalty received its greatest test.

The Metis, under Louis Riel, had taken up arms and rebelled against the new dominion. The Cree had joined them, and strong pressure was on all the Indians of the west — many of them embittered by broken white promises — to join in the rebellion.

All through Alberta, as the rebellion grew in strength and ferocity, Indian agents, missionaries and red-coated mounties struggled to hold the plains Indians in check.

It was a tense situation. There was no question of how Crowfoot himself felt, but the great chief was now aging, and the young sometimes will not heed the words of the old.

Then, in Parliament on April 12, during debate on

the rebellion, the prime minister Sir John A. Macdonald rose to speak.

"I have received a telegram signed by Crowfoot, which I will read.

It is not in Blackfoot:

"From Blackfoot Crossing, via Gleichen, N.W.T., 11th April, 1885:

"On behalf of myself and people I wish to send through you to the Great Mother the words I have given to the Governor at a Council here, at which all my minor chiefs and young men were present. We are agreed and determined to remain loyal to the Queen. Our young men will go to work on the reserves and will raise all the crops they can, and we hope the Government will help us to sell what we cannot use . . .

"Should any Indians come to our reserve and ask us to join them in war we will send them away . . .

"The words I sent by Father Lacombe I again send: We will be loyal to the Queen whatever happens. I have a copy of this, and when the trouble is over will have it with pride to show to the Queen's officers: and we leave our future in your hands . . .

"Crowfoot."

Once more the prairie leader had succeeded, and once more he had prevented an alliance that would have taken a bloody toll of Alberta's white people.

Crowfoot, chief of all the Blackfoot and keeper of the peace. A man who made one promise — "We will be loyal to the Queen whatever happens"— and never broke it.

* * * *

EMPEROR PICK, THE BOTTLE KING . . .

By 1916, despite the sorrow of the war in Europe, Albertans had every reason to be pleased with the quality of law and order in their province.

The mounties had done their job well. No one worried any more about Indian problems or unrestrained violence or wolfers from the Montana side of the border.

And in town after growing town, municipal police forces were building a system of law enforcement that would preserve the redcoat traditions of justice.

But then, on July 1, 1916, all that changed. Prohibition came to Alberta and, within months, Alberta would be caught up in nightmare — sometimes tragic and sometimes comic — that would shatter the peace for six long years.

It was a strange world, filled with reckless men racing big black cars across the prairie nights, with rural milkmen whose big cans gurgled with something that was decidedly not milk, with box cars filled with "pickled pork" — hog carcasses stuffed to the snout with bottles of bootleg booze.

It was a world where even the janitor of a respectable Baptist church in Calgary thought nothing of converting the building's basement to a distillery.

Everything seems to have gone just a little crazy. When, a matter of months after that July 1, the mounties withdrew their protection from rural Alberta and the short-lived Alberta Provincial Police force took over, people just shook their heads philosophically.

Even when the battles between bootlegger and police began to cost lives, Alberta people could not shake the feeling that it was all not quite real, that it was just a weird game soon to be called on account of foolishness.

"I've been drinking beer since I was old enough to jump over a miner's lamp," a boozer named Joe Perotte had announced on the eve of prohibition, "and I'm damned if I'm gonna stop now." There was many an Albertan who felt the same way.

For the police, it was the worst of all possible situations. No matter how talented they were, or how devoted, there was just no way to enforce impossible laws — particularly when most of the population was bent on obstructing the enforcement of those laws.

Which brings us to Emperor Pick, a man whose story sums up all the unreality and tragedy of those unreal and tragic years.

Every age in history seems to create a man especially suited to it — and Emilio Picariello was the ideal man for the age of prohibition.

Born in Sicily in 1875, the big, smiling Italian came to Canada at the turn of the century. After working in the east for a few years — and getting married — he came west, settling first in Fernie, B.C. and finally in Blairmore as owner of the Alberta Hotel.

Prohibition seemed to Picariello to be the chance of a lifetime. In Fernie, in addition to building up a legitimate business in macaroni and ice cream, he had become the local distributor for a wine company. He had also begun the strange occupation of collecting bottles.

Hiding behind his smile, Mr. Pick had quietly cornered the market in bottles. On Sept. 22, 1916, he advertised the astonishing fact he had 27,000 bottles for sale: quarts 40 cents and pints 22 cents a dozen.

Before long every paper in the Crows Nest Pass was carrying another Pick advertisement that read: "E. Pick, the Bottle King, requests that all persons selling bottles hold them until they see E. Pick, who pays top prices."

Within weeks, most breweries were relying on Pick's efficient bottle-gathering system rather than trying to collect their own or buy new ones.

Looking over the prohibition scene, Pick made the purchase of the Alberta Hotel in Blairmore. Then he negotiated a deal that made him sole agent of Lethbridge Brewery products in the Crows Nest and began advertising "temperance" beer — a product that looked like beer, even tasted vaguely like beer, but that sure wasn't beer in any real sense of the name.

The combination of hotel, bottles and near-beer gave Pick the "front" he wanted. He was ready to go into the bootleg business.

Late in 1918, he bought a fleet of Model T Fords, and fitted them with barrier-busting bumpers made from steel pipe filled with concrete.

In the basement of the Alberta hotel, he dug a small room in one wall, then extended a tunnel from this room out under the roadway. The entrance to the sideroom was covered with a rough curtain of burlap, in front of which were stacked huge barrels of his famous 40-ounce bottles.

The bottles in the barrels were empty, but the ones packed into the hiding place on the other side of the burlap screen were not.

Pick's favorite method of bringing in supplies was to use truckloads of flour. The outer layers of sacks contained flour — in case of a search — but all the rest of the sacks were filled with bottles of booze.

The police were on to Emperor Pick — as he was becoming known — right from the start. But they couldn't catch him. His hiding places were too good, his operation too well set up. And the people of Blairmore were bent on protecting him.

The last fact was due to Emperor Pick's growing reputation as a philanthropist. Partly because he really was a kindly man, and partly because he was a shrewd businessman, Pick devoted himself to good works. He subscribed for $50,-000 in Canadian Victory Bonds, he gave freely to the poor at Christmas time, and he was always there with an open pocket when someone needed help.

On the rare occasion when a police raid on his near-beer warehouse turned up a keg or two that was over-strength, Pick went to court and paid his fines without a whimper — and with a bow of acknowledgement to the talent of the police.

Emperor Pick might have survived the prohibition era — as did some other Alberta bootleggers — and become a "respectable" businessman.

But, on Sept. 21, 1922, fate dealt Pick a cruel hand, and justice finally caught up with him.

On that day, Const. R. M. Day of the provincial police at Blairmore was tipped-off that Mr. Pick was going to Fernie, B.C. for a load of whiskey.

About 4 o'clock, an A.P.P. officer named Steve Lawson and Police Chief James Houghton watched Pick's cavalcade of three cars come along the main street of Coleman. At the wheel of the first was the emperor's mechanic, J. J. McAlpine; driving the second was Pick's son, Steve, 19. The emperor himself drove the third.

Word was flashed to Sgt. James Scott at Blairmore. He and Const. Day were waiting at the Alberta Hotel when Pick's party arrived.

Mr. Pick was walking up to the hotel when the two officers appeared and served him with a search warrant. Pick turned abruptly and dashed for his car. He jammed down the horn in a warning signal and the police saw young Steve roar off in his souped-up McLaughlin.

Sgt. Scott rushed for his car and gave chase. But by this time Mr. Pick was also on the road, blocking Scott as he tried to catch up to young Steve.

Time and again Scott tried to pass, and time and again was cut off by Mr. Pick's swerving car. Scott finally had to abandon the chase.

In Coleman, warned by phone that Steve was on the way, Const. Lawson was waiting in the street to stop him. Steve, however, didn't stop. He swerved by the waiting policeman and Lawson began firing at the car. One shot hit Steve in the hand, but he kept going and made good his escape towards Michel.

By the time he returned to Blairmore, Mr. Pick had learned of Steve's wounding. Met at the hotel by Sgt. Scott, he is said to have grinned and remarked: "I saved my load, anyway, and I don't care how many times I ditch you. It was lucky for Lawson that he did not kill my boy, or else I would kill him."

Later that night, Pick learned Steve had been arrested. For some reason, he decided to go to Coleman and confront Lawson.

With him he took Florence Lassandro, the 22-year-old wife of a friend.

Pick stopped his car in front of the police barracks and Lawson came out. The policeman stood, with one foot on the running-board, talking to Pick.

Mrs. Lassandro later reported that Pick told the officer, "You shot my boy and you're going with me to get him." An argument followed and, for some reason, Pick drew a gun.

In the struggle several shots were fired, tearing through the windshield and dashboard of the car.

At one point, the muzzle swung towards Mrs. Lassandro, who had drawn a gun of her own by now. In a panic, she fired. Lawson fell to the road and was dead in a matter of minutes.

Pick and Mrs. Lassandro were arrested at Blairmore the following day.

The two were tried for murder, found guilty and, on May 3, 1923 — barely a year before the repeal of prohibition — they were hanged at Fort Saskatchewan.

Today, every so often, one of Mr. Pick's famous green 40-ounce bottles will turn up. Not much of a monument for an emperor — or an era.

* * * *

THE GREAT DEFENDER . . .

Bob Edwards, editor of Calgary's famous Eye Opener, once described Paddy Nolan, K.C., as "one of the seven wonders of the world."

There's no question that he was that and — in terms of Alberta justice — maybe more. Paddy Nolan was the greatest, and wittiest, criminal lawyer in Alberta history; possibly in Canadian history.

The facts of his life are straightforward enough. He was born Patric James Nolan in Limerick, Ireland, on St. Patrick's Day, 1864.

Educated in law, he practised in Ireland and in England before coming to Alberta — then simply the North West Territories — in 1889.

He had the unique distinction of having been admitted to three bars: the Bar of Ireland, the Bar of England, and the Bar of the N.W.T.

But here is where Nolan himself takes over. Once, when

reference to his triple admittance was made, Nolan solemnly assured his audience that the reference was an understatement. "In fact," he beamed, "I've made it a point to be admitted to every bar that would open its doors to me — and it was more than three I assure you!"

Paddy Nolan was a man who inspired stories by the dozens and hundreds and many of these stories have survived.

So here, in the hope they may contain a trace of quicksilver, are a few of the more famous stories about Paddy Nolan.

* * * *

Of all the breeds of law-breakers, none was closer to Nolan's heart than the cattle rustler. And when someone was close to Nolan's heart, as his records show, that someone usually got acquitted. Indeed, so good was Paddy at defending rustlers that the Stockmen's Association tried to hire him as their special prosecutor — just to have him on their side for a change.

On one occasion, Nolan was defending a man accused of stealing a steer from the ranch of W.R. Hull, a wealthy cattleman who lived in Calgary and had his spread 70 miles away in Claresholm.

Hull knew nothing of the details of the case. He had been called by the Crown simply to prove his ownership of the animal.

When Nolan rose to cross-examine, he nodded politely to Hull and asked: "I believe you are one of the largest ranchers in Alberta, Mr. Hull?"

"Yes, Mr. Nolan, I believe I am."

"And where are your headquarters, Mr. Hull?"

"In Calgary, Mr. Nolan."

"And where are your hindquarters, Mr. Hull?"

"In Claresholm, Mr. Nolan," Hull responded before he could stop himself.

"Well," said Nolan drawing back to beam at the jury, "if your headquarters are in Calgary and your hindquarters are in Claresholm, you are certainly the very largest rancher in Alberta!"

* * * *

Nolan's client was a poor Calgary widow who, being left penniless, had tried to raise a few dollars by raffling off her late husband's watch — and suddenly found herself charged with conducting a lottery.

Nolan knew, according to the letter of the law at least, the woman was guilty. But he was incensed at the injustice of the situation.

So, a few days before the case was to come to trial,

Nolan went to visit the judge who was to try the woman — with the full knowledge that the judge hadn't yet been informed he'd be hearing the case.

Nolan poured out a tale of woe about the woman's pitiable condition and the judge, moved to compassion, bought two raffle tickets which Nolan just happened to have with him.

Later, the squirming judge listened as the prosecution proved its charge beyond any shadow of a doubt, then listened as the twinkling-eyed Nolan summed up his arguments for the defence:

"Your Honor knows full well the danger of these lotteries, and how even the best-intentioned people in the community fall victim to them and, out of sheer sympathy for their object, commit offences by buying tickets in them — as no doubt Your Honor has done on occasion yourself."

The woman was given a suspended sentence.

* * * *

For all his talent as a lawyer, Nolan didn't win all his cases — nor did he expect to. But he suffered one legal defeat he never forgot — in a murder trial that is still one of the most famous and controversial in Alberta court history.

It was the trial of a young man named Ernest Cashel.

Cashel was a Wyoming cowboy who had fled to Alberta with a posse at his heels. Arriving in Red Deer, he made friends with an old homesteader and arranged to spend the winter with him.

One day, Cashel appeared at a bank in Red Deer and had a hundred dollar bill changed into smaller bills.

There was a peculiar blue smudge on a corner of the bill, and the teller recognized it as one he'd paid out to the old homesteader some weeks before.

"Where'd you get this?" the teller asked, more curious

than suspicious. Cashel responded simply that he got it from a man with whom he was staying.

Shortly after, Cashel disappeared from Red Deer. He appeared in Calgary and passed a bad cheque; an act that brought him to the attention of the police. A warrant was issued and the North West Mounted Police caught up with Cashel in Moose Jaw.

As Cashel, under guard, was being brought back to Calgary, he jumped through the window of the train and escaped.

In Red Deer, meanwhile, some neighbors had discovered that the old homesteader was missing, and had informed the police.

As the search was going on, the teller who had changed the bill for Cashel opened a copy of The Calgary Herald one day and discovered a picture of the man and the story of his daring escape from the train.

The teller immediately hurried to the police with his story of the hundred dollar bill and the searches for both Cashel and the old homesteader were intensified.

The police found the body of the old man when the spring break-up came. There were marks of violence on the corpse. A warrant was sworn out for Cashel's arrest on the charge of murder.

Cashel was finally found on a ranch in Saskatchewan, and brought to Calgary to stand trial.

Nolan undertook the defence. The case was circumstantial, but it was damning — particularly in the light of Cashel's reputation and his previous escape.

Those who were at the trial claim that Nolan never worked harder at a case in his life, but it was all in vain. Cashel was found guilty and sentenced to hang.

Nolan was a stubborn Irishman. Determined not to give

up, and with the hanging only days away, he hurried to Ottawa to appeal to the justice minister for a new trial.

Nolan had already started the interview with the minister when a telegram arrived for him. He read it, then crumpled it in a ball, and heaved a sigh of defeat.

"Never mind the new trial," he said. "My client has escaped."

The night before, Cashel's brother had smuggled two guns into the death cell and, holding three guards at gunpoint, Cashel had got away.

It took time, but Cashel was eventually caught, and with Nolan now powerless to help, duly hung.

To this day, there are those who argue that Cashel was innocent, and that Nolan would somehow have proved it if his client hadn't made that escape from the death cell.

There is no doubt how Nolan felt about it. The night Cashel was executed, Nolan was playing a gloomy game of billiards in the Royal Hotel in Calgary when the hangman accidentally walked in.

Enraged, Nolan took off after him with a billiard cue and only the efforts of the bystanders spared the executioner from a savage beating.

But the story of Paddy Nolan shouldn't end on so angry a note.

When Nolan died in 1913, at the too-young age of 49, The Calgary Herald found a much more fitting way to bring his story to a close:

"His remarkable skills as a barrister, his marvellous and never-failing wit, his pungency of criticism and his warmth of praise, have been known those many years. Stories were told of him around the world, each one testifying to the breadth of his Irish kindness, and to the marvellous flow of his Irish humor . . ."

* * * *

ONE LAST WORD OF JUSTICE . . .

Inevitably, in the history of every place, there is one incident, sometimes small, that sums up the worth of its system of law and justice.

In Alberta, the incident came in 1899 when three Indians from Lesser Slave Lake were arrested and brought to trial for murder.

The case, from both the Indian and white points of view, was simple. To the Indian mind, the three had done a duty to their people. To the white, it was a case of cold-blooded homicide.

An Indian named The Pheasant had run amuck in his tribe's camp, threatening to kill and eat anyone who crossed his path.

This sort of thing had happened before, to other men, and the Cree believed that The Pheasant was possessed of a cannibal spirit known as the Witigo which prompted him to eat his own kind.

The medicine men of the tribe tried to drive the spirit out, but to no avail.

Finally three executioners were chosen, and they cut The Pheasant down with their war axes, then opened his body to let out the evil spirit.

When the Mounted Police heard what had happened, they arrested the three and took them to Edmonton to stand trial.

A missionary working among the Cree, Father Falher, saw the extenuating circumstances of the case and wrote to Father Lacombe, asking him to plead the Indians' case to the courts.

This he did. It says something important about the humanity of justice in Alberta to record that all three were released and allowed to return to their own people.

* * * *

HEALER & HELPER

"In 1880, he heeded the call of the west, joined the North West Mounted Police force with a group of other young men from the east, and was sent to the North West Territories. They travelled via the U.S. on flat boats up the Missouri River to Fort Benton, thence on to Fort Walsh . . .

"At Fort Benton, an amusing incident occurred. All the boys were broke. Fort Benton was then a frontier town with few service facilities. One resourceful young chap, who was a barber by trade, put up a chair on the sidewalk and a sign nearby that read BARBER. Soon he was very busy, and the money began to roll in.

"Not to be outdone, Fred Shaw put up a sign on the sidewalk reading DENTIST, set out a chair and soon the extracted teeth were strewn about the board walk." (A pioneer's recollection of Dr. Frederick D. Shaw, first registered dentist in Alberta.)

* * * *

FRANK MEWBURN, SURGEON . . .

Of all the great medical men who came to frontier Alberta, one is consistently singled out as "the Alberta doctor".

It's not that Dr. Frank Hamilton Mewburn was the best surgeon in the world, or that he headed off some grave epidemic.

It's just that, in this frail little doctor, strength, compassion and humor were blended in exactly the right proportions to let him face harsh and primitive conditions, and triumph.

The Lethbridge that Dr. Mewburn found in 1885 was about as primitive, in the medical sense, as he'd ever seen.

All medical care was being provided by the town druggist, who would examine patients, carefully write out a list of the symptoms, then mail the list to the NWMP doctor in Fort Macleod for a diagnosis!

Fortunately, as nearly as we can make out from history, all the patients were hardy enough to survive the wait.

Needless to say, everyone — particularly the druggist — was delighted to have Dr. Mewburn in town. The delight persisted even though the new doctor somehow managed to lose the first patient he treated.

The patient, a Swedish miner, had complained vaguely of some internal disorder which Dr. Mewburn couldn't pin down. The next morning, the miner was found dead in his bunk.

The man's superintendent tried to soothe Mewburn by pointing out that: "Well, doctor, we all must die sometime or another, and some pass away no matter how we may try to prevent it.

"It cannot, therefore, be avoided, so there is no use worrying over it."

To which Dr. Mewburn responded with an explosive "Doesn't that beat hell!"

The new doctor, people gathered, had a philosophical streak in him.

One of the biggest tests the pioneer doctor faced was the treatment of Indian patients. It wasn't just a problem of overcoming their primitive fears; it was also a problem of persuading them to part with a fee.

Dr. Mewburn met both problems almost right away, and solved both — with a little help — just as quickly.

The first Indian patient he treated was a man from the Blood reserve who arrived at his surgery surrounded by a flock of worried relatives.

Mewburn quickly diagnosed the man's condition as a severe goitre, and he knew he'd have to operate. He turned to face the Indian's relatives and delivered a solemn speech:

"I shall have to make a big cut. If you all do as I tell you after the big cut is made, this man may get well, but I cannot tell for sure until I have made the big cut, and then if he does not get well, and if he should die, you must not blame me.

"What do you say? Shall I make the big cut?"

His audience — including the man who would have to undergo the "big cut" — all grunted eager agreement.

The operation was a success and the man recovered completely. From that point on, Mewburn had the total trust of the Indians and the Bloods, and every other tribe in the Blackfoot confederacy made a point of bringing all their seriously ill people to him for treatment.

The second problem — that of collecting fees — was solved with the kind assistance of the Indian agents.

One day, an aged squaw appeared in Mewburn's office

with a little girl — and a note which she handed to the doctor.

The note read: "Dear Dr. Mewburn; This old woman has a little girl with her who has a large lump on her neck, which she would like you to remove. Also, the old lady has in her pocket a lump of twenty-five dollars which she would like to have removed at the same time." The note was signed by an Indian agent.

Both operations were performed successfully.

Dr. Mewburn would treat any kind of ailment, but his real love was surgery. And it was in the operating theatre that he created his reputation as one of the west's most volatile characters.

Indeed, the only time he was ever known to take an operating-room incident calmly was a day when all the lights went out during an operation. As the nurses and assistants winced and braced themselves for the inevitable outburst, all they got was the gentle protest that "I can't do the subject justice."

That occasion, however, was the exception. Once, for example, Mrs. Mewburn tried to telephone him while he was in the operating room.

Mewburn stormed out, had a nurse hold up the receiver so he wouldn't have to touch it with his sterilized gloves, and yelled: "Is that you, Louise? Go to h--l!" He then returned to finish the operation.

Probably the most famous illustration of Mewburn temper is the one recorded by John Higinbotham in his book, When the West Was Young:

"During a 'Mission' at which a number of the Roman Catholic clergy, bishops and priests, from various parts of Alberta gathered at Macleod, one of the visiting fathers, who was over eighty years of age, was suddenly stricken with a strangulated hernia.

"Dr. G.A. Kennedy was called in, but feared to operate owing to the patient's advanced age. He telephoned to Lethbridge for Dr. Mewburn and the latter immediately responded by Mounted Police conveyance.

"He decided to operate at once by local anaesthetic and arranged that one of the bishops (Legal, I think it was) should read to the patient and thus divert his mind during the operation.

"In the midst of the clinic a fly entered the room and buzzed so close to the operating table that it got on Dr. Mewburn's nerves. His lips began to move convulsively yet he continued with difficulty to work without exploding.

"Finally, as the objectionable intruder persisted in annoying him, he looked at Dr. Kennedy, who shook his head as a warning to the 'Chief' to contain himself, and said, 'Kennedy, kill that fly or put the bishop out, I don't give a damn which, as I can't hold myself any longer.'

"I never learned whether the fly was swatted or the bishop made his exit."

Mewburn was a tireless worker. At no time in his life was he ever known to refuse an appeal for help, no matter what the weather or time of day. Nor was he ever known to make any distinction between rich and poor. He treated both alike, and never pressed a man for payment. When the Galt Hospital was opened in Lethbridge, Dr. Mewburn became its first superintendent.

And, for all his legendary temper, Mewburn was basically a gentle man. When, in 1929, he was in a hospital bed dying of pneumonia, one of the last things he said to his nurse was:

"I hope my going won't give you too much trouble . . ."

As we said at the beginning, it's not that Dr. Frank Hamilton Mewburn was the best surgeon in the world, or that he headed off some grave epidemic.

It's just that, well, he was "the Alberta doctor".

* * * *

The history of Alberta is filled with the names of helpers. On the frontier, everyone was everyone's neighbor, and his sole protection against the dangers of a new land.

Help took many forms. In Red Deer, for instance, it was four young bachelors who raised the first building there — then cheerfully went to work to help every new arrival raise a home for himself.

Or it was a handful of boy scouts who cornered and captured a bank robber and held him until the police arrived. One of those boys, by the way, was a youngster named Roland Michener — who went on to become our Governor-General.

Once it was Father Lacombe, who nearly died when he chose to starve rather than keep his slim provisions from 18 dying Indians.

And once it was John Ware, the pioneer rancher, who demonstrated that "help" doesn't always turn out to be what you might expect.

Ware had ridden out one day to see a neighbor on business. He reached the house to find the man away — and his wife in the midst of having a baby.

Ware had no choice but to roll up his sleeves and help. When the immediate crisis had been handled, Ware rode back and fetched some female assistance for the new mother.

Then he rode into town to "break" the news to the new father.

He found the man propped up at the bar, having a few to steady his nerves.

"I'm going to teach you your duty to your family," Ware informed him grimly, then gave the man a sound thrashing.

The unhappy gentleman carried around the bruises of Ware's "helping hand" long enough to make sure that he became one of the most devoted of husbands.

But there were just too many helpers, and too many occasions on which they helped, to tell the whole story. So, instead, we'll tell just two stories — one of a little man and one of a little girl — and hope they'll show how many things the word "help" can really mean.

* * * *

THE "WORTHLESS" ONE . . .

His name was Henry Collins and he lived 86 years. In his prime, he weighed more than 180 pounds and was so strong that he lifted a 400-pound bale of goods.

But Henry Collins was only four feet tall, a dwarf, and the name given him by his Cree mother's people was "Muchias, the Worthless One".

No name was ever further from the character of the man who carried it.

Even in Edmonton, where there are still some who remember Muchias by sight, it may come as a surprise to think of him as a "helper".

But he was a helper, one of the finest on the frontier.

Orphaned at the age of nine, Muchias was adopted by John Walter of the Hudson's Bay Company, and came with the Walter family to the tiny settlement of Edmonton.

If anyone was inclined to feel pity for Muchias when they saw him first, Muchias quickly disinclined them. He had a ready grin and the ability to laugh at himself. And, as he used to point out, he was really only a dwarf from the hips down. The rest of him was full-sized. He used to brag that, if it weren't for his legs, he'd be seven and a half feet tall.

Into the harshness of frontier life, Muchias injected a valuable commodity — laughter.

And, right from the first, Muchias was convinced that his role in life was to help those around him. He became Edmonton's water man, beaming out from under a white stetson and carrying heavy pails into every kitchen in town.

If there was a woman who needed wood chopped, Muchias would appear out of nowhere and chop it — without asking for so much as a thank-you. And if a man had a heavy load to move, Muchias was there to help move it.

He helped put houses up and, in time of flood, he helped chain them down. He hunted and fished, and shared what he got with anyone who needed it.

And more than all this — much more — he helped the children of Edmonton.

Muchias was child-sized and, at a spot close to where Edmonton's high-level bridge now stands, he created a child-sized house and opened its doors to all the children in town.

For a generation of Edmonton children, chafing in the confinement of a rough settlement, Muchias became the magic guide to a magic world.

As Tony Cashman, author of The Edmonton Story, put it: "The house of a friendly dwarf, set in the woods, something right out of a fairy tale."

Child-like himself, Muchias loved the children. He let them run free in the house, and they marvelled at the miniature furniture and utensils. When they were tired, they'd sit with Muchias and tell him stories, or listen to the stories he had to tell.

With his busy hands, he made miniature bows and arrows for the boys, and carved toys and trinkets for the girls.

Muchias gave a strong and helping hand to a city, and brought laughter and magic to a generation of children for whom laughter and magic were scarce and precious.

There are still a lot of grey-haired "children" in Edmonton today who are grateful to the "worthless one" for that.

* * * *

THE FROST-BITTEN "FEAT". . .

"Heroism may be found anywhere," the Pembina News Adviser noted on Jan. 6, 1965.

It wasn't meant as a belittling statement. Far from it. It was an awed tribute to a 4½-year-old heroine named Doris Pollard.

The ultimate of help is always heroism and, in this sense, Doris represents one of the ultimate helpers.

Doris, a two-year-old brother, a three-year-old brother, and a nine-month-old baby sister were alone in their farm home near Chip Lake one morning just before Christmas.

Doris' parents were in the barn with a veterinarian, discussing the condition of a sick animal.

Doris was in the kitchen, drying a dish, when the stove that heated the farm house exploded and filled the house with flames.

The little girl ran into a back room where her younger brothers were playing. She grabbed their hands and led them through the flames to the crib where nine-month-old Sharon was sleeping. Doris pulled up a stool and, stretching, reached in and lifted out the baby.

Then, carrying Sharon in her arms and herding the two boys ahead of her, she struggled out of the house.

Behind her, as she waded bare-foot through the snow, the farm house was already an inferno. In a matter of minutes, even before her parents could run up from the barn, the house was destroyed.

Doris ended up in Drayton Valley Municipal Hospital with frost-bitten feet.

She didn't stay there long. And, in a matter of a few months, she was receiving a tribute to her courage.

For saving the lives of the three children, the Alberta Weekly Newspaper editors had named her the winner of a special award for heroism — the only special award ever — and named her the youngest Alberta Junior Citizen of the Year in history.

It could be that award was the first document in a new and exciting chapter of our Alberta heritage . . .

CONDENSED BIBLIOGRAPHY

Aberhart of Alberta, by L. P. V. Johnson & Ola MacNutt
Alberta Folklore, by Brian McMullin
Alberta's Petroleum Paternity, by Floyd K. Beach
Battle at Belly River, compiled by Alexander Johnson
Big Valley Story, compiled by Mrs. Gordon Fowler
Bill Miner: Train Robber, by Frank W. Anderson
Blackfeet Tales of Glacier National Park, by J. W. Shultz
Blackfoot Ghost Dance, by Hugh A. Dempsey
Blackfoot Shaking Tent, by Claude E. Schaeffer
Blackfoot Winter Count, by Hugh A. Dempsey
Boats and Barges on The Belly, by Historical Society of Alberta
Buchanan of Lethbridge, by Charles Frank Steel
Calgary-Banff Highway, by Frontier
Calgary Cavalcade, by Grant MacEwan
Canadian Rockies, by Esther Fraser
Cypress Hills, by Tom Primrose
Early History of the Medicine Hat Country, by J. W. Morrow
Edmonton, A History, by J. D. McGregor
Edmonton Story, by Tony Cashman
Enchanted Banff and Lake Louise, by Frontier
Ethnic Furniture, by Hugh A. Dempsey
Eye Opener Bob, by Grant MacEwan
Foot Prints of The Gaetz Family, by Annie L. Gaetz
Fort Macleod, edited by H. G. Long
Frank Slide Story, by Frank W. Anderson
Frontier Days in Leduc and District
Glenbow Collects, by Lorne E. Render
Grande Prairie, Capitol of the Peace, by Isabel M. Campbell
Great Canadian Oil Patch, by Earle Gray
Historic Sites of Alberta, pub. by Government of Alberta
History of Early Edmonton, by Beatrice Ockley
History of The Province of Alberta, by Archibald MacRae
History of Red Deer, by Wellington Dawe
History of St. Paul, by the St. Paul Journal
Impact of Oil, by Earle Gray
Incredible Rogers Pass, by Frontier
Indian and the Horse, by F. G. Roe
Indian Chiefs, Ancient and Modern, by Samuel Middleton
Indian Days in the Canadian Rockies, by Marius Barbeau
Indian Days on the Western Prairies, by Marius Barbeau
Indian Names for Alberta Communities, by Hugh A. Dempsey
Indians: Their Manners and Customs, by John McLean
Jerry Potts, Plainsman, by Hugh A. Dempsey
Lost Lemon Mine, by Riley, Primrose and Dempsey

More Edmonton Stories, by Tony Cashman
Opening the Great West, by Rev. John McDougall
Park Country, by Annie L. Gaetz
Pas-ka-poo, by The Rimbey Record
Picturesque Cardston and Environments
Pioneer Days of Hanna and District
Ponoka
Roamin' Empire, by Ken Liddell
Romantic Crow's Nest Pass, by Frontier
Rum Runners, by Frank W. Anderson
Saamis, The Medicine Hat, by Sen. F. W. Gershaw
St. Albert, by Emile Tardif, o.m.i.
Sergeant Harry Morren, by Frank W. Anderson
Seventy South Alberta Years, by S. Evangeline Warren
Tatanga Mani, by Grant MacEwan
Waterton, Land of Leisure, by Frontier
West of The Sea, by Grant MacEwan
When The West Was Young, by John D. Higinbotham
Where Waters Flow, pub. by the Town of Vauxhall